WHERE THE SEARCH LEADS TO LIFE

All Scripture quotations, unless otherwise indicated, are taken from the Holy
Bible: New International Version, © 1973, 1978, 1984 by the International Bible
Society, Published by Zondervan Bible Publishers, Grand Rapids, Michigan.

Printed in the United States of America

Published by Life ConneXions
The Publishing Group of Campus Crusade for Christ
375 Highway 74 South, Suite A
Peachtree City, GA 30269
To Order: 408.358.3470

ISBN 13: 9781563993046
ISBN 10: 1-56399-304X

CONTENTS

*"I really need help in my life. I have
been lost for a long time."*

— D., Namibia —

*"It is not the will of my Father
who is in heaven that one of these
little ones should perish."*

— Matthew 18:14 —

Dear Global Media Outreach Partner

This book represents just a tiny sampling of responses from people all across the world, from every nation. Their comments demonstrate two significant truths:

First, the greatest issue facing mankind is spiritual emptiness. It manifests itself in deep depression, anxieties, addictions, broken relationships, anger, hate, violence, and the darkness so many face in an increasingly chaotic world.

Second, spiritual emptiness leads to a hunger to know God. They arrive from every country, in many languages, and regardless of culture or economic standing, their heart-cry is,

"Can you help me know God?"

Not knowing how to accomplish this, they come to us—in a safe place, a place of "anonymous intimacy"—where they can share their burdens, their guilt, their deepest concerns.

Automated responses do not touch the soul of someone who is crying for help. We believe the only way to effectively minister is through person-to-person contact, expressing compassion, and through the power of prayer to bring seekers to the foot of Calvary's cross. That's why we have trained and mobilized thousands of Online Missionaries, mostly laypeople, to carry out this ministry.

As people encounter the Savior, their burdens begin to lift, and they start on the journey to the joyful and abundant life He promised. In these pages you'll meet some of those who have found the answer, and are stepping out of the darkness into a Spirit-filled life of meaning and purpose.

It is our extraordinary privilege to provide highly personal, gut-level ministry to so many in need from every nation. We are the first generation to hold in our hands the technology to give everyone on earth multiple opportunities to know Jesus. This is the Internet moment in human history. We have never seen an opportunity like this—to truly reach the entire world for Christ.

In response to the disciples' question:

"What will be the sign of your coming at the end of the age?"

Jesus replied,

"This gospel of the kingdom will be preached in the whole world as a witness to all nations . . . and then the end shall come." *(Matt. 24:14)*

Through Global Media Outreach websites, Internet Radio, GMO-TV on demand, and the Mobile (cell phone) Outreach Center, tens of millions are currently receiving the gospel across the entire world. Not a single nation is without witness. The technology to accomplish the task is not a distant dream. It is in our hands—today!

Blessings,

Walt Wilson
Global Media Outreach
Founder & Chairman

Good News

Every Second

"I've been a sinner in the eyes of Christ for my deeds. I therefore, repented from wrongdoings. I wish to follow Christ as my personal Savior."

— Kur, Sudan —

Around the Clock

"Jesus said, 'All authority has been given to Me in heaven and on earth. Go therefore and make disciples of all the nations, baptizing them in the name of the Father and the Son and the Holy Spirit, teaching them to observe all that I commanded you . . ."

— Matthew 28:18–20 —

Around the World

Every Day, Two Million People Search The Internet For God, For Meaning, For Hope

People in astonishing numbers are turning to the Internet searching for answers. Authorities estimate that every day, more than two million people search the Internet for God, for spiritual guidance, for hope.

These are not just statistics—they're men, women, and young people who are struggling, searching, trying to connect, trying to find something to fill the emptiness inside.

The people of God urgently need to be at these ever-widening crossroads. We must do everything we can to respond to those who are searching. We must work together to share with them the hope of Jesus, and connect new believers to caring Christian workers who can disciple them.

"I have never been a Christian. I was born and raised as an atheist. Your simple message that I found by googling "Jesus" and pressing "feeling lucky" led me to your website. It answered some basic questions for me. Did I get lucky? Why is Jesus calling to me now? I have heard His voice, and received an invitation that I did not ask for. I must now turn to those living for more answers, so that I might find what I have always sought. I just prayed to receive Christ as my Savior for the first time."

— Everett, USA —

Searching

"I'm ready to accept Jesus Christ into my life. So many bad things are happening to my family right now. I don't know where else to turn . . . I can't fight it anymore."

— H., Louisiana —

For God

For Meaning

"My wife and I are at our wits' end. We have had one misfortune after another for the last two years, but have always struggled through. Today, however, was the worst with one thing after another all at once. My wife was crying and said she was sick of living in this hell. I instantly thought of something my brother had said to me a while back. He had said he was living in hell until he got saved. I called my brother today and was telling him about today's misfortune, and he said I would feel so much better if I gave my life over to Jesus. So I googled the sinner's prayer and ended up on your website. My wife and I both said the prayer and would really like to be more educated, as neither one of us knows anything about Christianity or how to live the right way."

— John, New Hampshire —

For Hope

*"And this gospel of the kingdom will be preached
in all the world as a witness to every nation,
and then the end will come."*

— Matthew 24:14 NASB —

TO GIVE EVERY PERSON ON EARTH MULTIPLE
OPPORTUNITIES TO KNOW JESUS

Jesus2020: A Global Movement of Evangelism and Discipleship

The fields are white for harvest. Jesus said that. It's true. In the past four years, the response of people to the gospel through *Jesus2020* has been absolutely amazing.

People in spiritual crisis—in 195 countries—are hearing and responding to the gospel in unprecedented numbers.

Among those coming to faith are Buddhists, Hindus, Muslims, and those in the least reached, most inaccessible countries. This is a harvest opportunity of unparalleled magnitude and urgency. We praise God for the bounty of His Grace.

THAT THE WORLD MAY TRULY SEE

The Vision of *Jesus2020*

It is clear that God wants us to employ every available tool to present the gospel to every person on earth.

In His hands, the innovative use of worldwide media platforms opens the widest possible door for the spread of the gospel in the 21st century. The unprecedented reach of global technology is our "Roman road," appointed by God for this hour in redemptive history.

With God's blessing, Global Media Outreach has become the leading digital-media pioneer in the world of missions (measured by the number of people who have indicated that they received Jesus). As a ministry, we are committed to sharing Jesus, making disciples, and drawing new believers from every nation into the family of God.

Our Goal is to:

- **Share** Jesus 100 billion times with searching people in every nation, giving every person on earth multiple opportunities to know and follow Jesus by 2020

- **See** 360 million people pray to receive Jesus Christ

- **Help** 100 million take foundational steps as followers of Jesus

- **Train** 100,000 online missionaries, supported by a prayer network of one million

The *Jesus2020* movement represents one of the most compelling discipleship breakthroughs to help fulfill the great commission in our time. It is possible.

Some will say, "It can't be done." The disciples could have said that when Jesus commanded them to preach the gospel to every creature. But they didn't. They knew that all things are possible through Christ who strengthens His people to accomplish the greatest enterprise in history for the glory of God.

"Seek the Lord while He may be found; Call upon Him while He is near. Let the wicked forsake his way, and the unrighteous man his thoughts; And let him return to the Lord, and He will have compassion on him . . . ."

— Isaiah 55:6–7 —

Arabic

English

Chinese

Every day around the world,
Jesus2020 is sharing the gospel in
11 major Internet trade languages.

German

ITALIAN

French

Japanese

Portuguese

These languages account for the majority
of all worldwide web activity.

RUSSIAN

Spanish

Swedish

English

English is the predominant language used throughout the world on the Internet. Eighty percent of the world's information is stored on computers in English.

www.Jesus2020.com

"I, too, am experiencing struggles in my life and want to welcome Jesus' presence and guidance in my life. I am Jewish and have experienced Jesus. As with your story, I need to take a leap of faith and surrender and know Jesus is here with me, guiding me and helping me; and it is my work to open to Him and accept Him."

— Linda, USA —

"I still have strongholds in my life. I don't know what to do. I feel that God can't forgive me for my sins. I desperately need help."

— Carl, USA —

"I need to talk to someone about a very bad experience I had; I don't know what I should do. I was raped and am now four months pregnant. Does God care? Can someone talk to me?"

— Young Woman, USA —

Arabic

There are 500 million Arabic-speaking people. *Jesus2020* is reaching them in 144 countries worldwide.

www.Almaseeh2020.com

"I have too much problems. I am sure my life will be 100% in danger if Muslim fundamentalists know about me. Mostly in nights I am reading your articles. I hope and pray for the coming of those days to go in churches and learn more about the holy religion of Christianity. Please do not forget me. I need your prayer."

— Ibrahim —

"When I accepted Jesus, I felt so much joy and peace. I need this for me forever. How?"

— Ishak, Egypt —

"How can I feel the touch of God on my life? I want to know God better."

— A., Syria —

"Those who have never been told about Him will see and those who have never heard of Him will understand."

— Isaiah 52:15 —

Results That Can be Verified and Reported to Our Partners

With proven capability and documented, metric-driven reporting—*Jesus2020's* global network is enabling multiple millions of people to discover and respond to the saving Good News of Jesus Christ.

Chinese

There are nearly 1.4 billion Chinese people around the world. The influence of the international Chinese community is felt on every continent.

www.Jesus2020.cn

"I am learning to understand the Lord and Christ, and wish to know more and how to start my prayers. Thanks for the advice."

— D., Singapore —

"I ask the Lord Jesus to guide and protect me from harm; strengthen my faith; give me long patience and an understanding heart."

— M., Taiwan —

"What do I need to be closer to God?"

— R., China —

Battle-Tested, Trustworthy—With a Growing Army of Trained Volunteers

• With 91 proven, Jesus-centered websites and 20 discipleship websites, *Jesus2020* continues to break new ground for the gospel worldwide. (A complete list of *Jesus2020* URLs is available upon request.)

• For those without Internet access, our communication platform for cell phone users is currently reaching hundreds of thousands of people each month.

• A grassroots movement of thousands of trained online missionary volunteers are helping these new believers take foundational steps in their journey with Jesus.

India

India is the second most populous country in the world, with 1.1 billion people. English is the co-official language of India.

www.Jesus2020.com

"I want to serve God—and I want to obtain that heavenly peace and happiness which I am lacking now."

— Niirmala, India —

"I am a Hindu who was suffering for so many years. That was hell for me. Two months ago, I started going to church and the Lord has brought me out of the pit from which I had fallen. My family and I will work for Christ till our last breath. We seek the Lord's blessings in this."

— Arasu, India —

"Please help me know more about Jesus Christ, and to reflect Him in my life to the rest of people to know His love."

— Paul, India —

The Capability to Reach Every Person on Earth

The number of people with cell phones will increase to 4.5 billion people by 2013. By 2020, there will be 8.5 billion people on earth. Right now, international telecommunications firms are working to connect everyone on earth with the internet by 2020 or sooner.

In a similar way, Jesus came in the fullness of time when the Greek language and Roman roads made it possible to access the entire population of the ancient world.

4.5 BILLION PEOPLE WILL HAVE CELL PHONES BY 2013

This means that in the 21st century—using all forms of worldwide communication technologies—God has made possible a revolutionary harvest. We now have the potential to impact the entire population of the world, adding to the church daily on a global scale never imagined before. We are the first generation in history to hold in our hands the technology capable of reaching every person on earth with the gospel.

It is Possible

In the 1920s, we doubted that radio would go global. It did. In the 1950s, we doubted that TV would be everywhere. It is.

In the 1990s we asked, "Could it be that one day everyone on earth will have access to the Internet?" The answer? Yes. It will reach every person, everywhere, to the very ends of the earth.

Has God ever failed to send messengers? Has He ever failed to provide the means to proclaim the glorious gospel of His Son?

Jesus said, "All authority has been given to me." That's why He commanded us to share the gospel with "every creature," and be "a witness to every nation."

He says to us simply, "Believe in God, believe also in Me." It is possible.

"Behold, I have made Him a witness to the peoples, a leader and commander for the peoples. Behold, you will call a nation you do not know, and a nation which knows you not will run to you, because of the Lord Your God, even the Holy One of Israel."

— Isaiah 55:4–5 —

Spanish

There are approximately 452 million Spanish-speaking people around the world, living in 22 Spanish-speaking countries. South America is the world's fastest-growing Internet region.

www.JesuCristo2020.com

"Thank you for your video, your disposition, and just for being here in the right moment in the right time."

— *G., Argentina* —

"I really want the Lord to make me the person He wants me to be. I love Him."

— *Marianela, Chile* —

"What if I sin a lot? I have thoughts—I can't get them out of my head even if I pray to God to help them get out, but they won't go away. Can I still have eternal life in Jesus?"

— *Ana, Mexico* —

Portuguese

There are 240 million Portuguese-speaking people around the world.

Portuguese is the official language in Brazil, Portugal, Angola, Mozambique, Cape Verde, São Tomé and Príncipe, Guinea-Bissau, East Timor, and Macau.

www.Jesus2020portugues.com

"Now I'm full of confidence in Jesus Christ that we are only saved by faith in Him, not by religion. I want to thank the team of Global Media Outreach for having sent me this e-mail, because that has helped me to be sure I'm going to the right path."

— R., Brazil —

Italian

The population of Italy is 59.5 million. However, Italian is also spoken in Switzerland, Croatia, Slovenia, and San Marino. Italian is the fourth largest language group in the European Union.

"I thank you for what you do to spread the word of God using today's technology. I found the prayer while I was looking on the Internet. I am a Catholic and I can never find the right words to say to Jesus, how my life was a disaster until I found Him. He gave me the real life. The suffering in my life is very strong, and trials too, but it's my heart that is changed. I want to tell other people that Jesus came to save us all, no matter in what situation we are. I hope you understand my English. Ciao from Sicily."

— Concetta, Italy —

Excellent
Kingdom Returns

"In difficult economic times, ministry partners must look for excellent Kingdom returns per dollar of contribution. Global Media Outreach offers you that kind of good stewardship opportunity."

— Steve Douglass, President, Campus Crusade for Christ —

"And the one on whom seed was sown on the good ground, this is the man who hears the word and understands it; who indeed bears fruit, and brings forth, some a hundredfold, some sixty, and some thirty."

— Matthew 13:23 —

Japanese

There are 130 million Japanese-speaking people in the world. Only one percent are Christian.

www.Jesus2020.jp

"I thank you for this message. I've never heard words of God before."

— K., Japan —

"I believe that God exists and Jesus redeemed our sins. After so many years of striving and failing, I learned how to surrender life to Jesus wholeheartedly. God bless this website."

— M., Japan —

"I want to develop a relationship with the Lord. I would like to learn how to pray consistently and meaningfully. Can you give me some pointers?"

— S., Japan —

French

There are 410 million French-speaking people around the world. French is an official language in 26 countries, and is spoken worldwide in 53 countries.

"I'm 32 years old and I've never been so lost in my life—I just want to give up and die. The only thing that keeps me going is my five-year-old son—I need help. I do not know how to start or what to do."

— Woman, Nice, France —

"How can I live with Jesus every day without leaving Him, in this difficult world, life of sins?"

— A., Rwanda —

"Please—I want to have Christ in my life. How can I pray hard to get Him so that He will forgive me my sin?"

— Emmanuel, Senegal —

Russian

In terms of geographical area, Russia is the largest country in the world with 143 million people, and millions more Russian speakers living in the countries of the former Soviet Union.

"I love our God Jesus Christ so much!! Thank you for kicking me out of the cold dead hands of sin!! I love you, Jesus!!"

— S., Russian Federation —

"I just prayed to receive Christ. What should I do next?"

— Konstantin, Russian Federation —

German

There are an estimated 96 million German speakers around the world. It is one of 23 official languages in the European Union.

www.Jesus2020.de

"Giving my life to Christ is the first step to the rest of my life. God Bless us all."

— G., Germany —

"Oh, it's good to have Christ in our soul, 'cause it is the only way we can see the truth and the light. I thank God for His precious mercy on me, 'cause I need Him more than I think."

— E., Germany —

Swedish

The population of Sweden is nine million. Fifty to eighty-five percent of Swedes are atheist, yet *Jesus2020* is reaching thousands of people each year with the gospel. We are also reaching Swedish speakers residing in 63 other countries.

www.Jesus2020sverige.com

"After a while of struggling, I recommitted my life to Christ, and want to live for Him full and true."

— A., Sweden —

"Becoming a follower of Jesus is the greatest thing that ever happened to me."

— D., Sweden —

"I am a Catholic priest but I want to receive Christ and I want God to be the central part of my life. Can you please help me?"

— Priest, Sweden —

Global Impact
for God's Glory

"I am not ashamed of the gospel, for it is the power of God for salvation to everyone who believes."

— Romans 1:16 —

This is just the beginning. The growth potential of *Jesus2020* is virtually unlimited.

We expect multiple millions more to gain access to the global network each and every year for decades to come. We must be ready to meet them at their crossroads, and offer them the hope and peace found only in the person and teaching of Jesus.

"Always be ready to give an answer to everyone who asks you to give an account for the hope that is in you."

— I Peter 3:15 —

Messages From Those Who are Coming to Jesus

You can imagine how exciting it is for our volunteer online missionaries to hear from—and personally interact with—the men and women who are coming to faith in Jesus. Every day around the world, *Jesus2020* is reaching people with the gospel in English, Arabic, Chinese, Spanish, Portuguese, Russian, Japanese, Italian, Swedish, French, and German.

"I am a disabled Marine, wounded in Iraq, and I want to get right with God. Can you send me anything that will help me get to know Jesus? I would be thankful."

U.S. Military Veteran

"I want to know God. I want to know Jesus. Will He forgive my sins for being a Muslim?"

Male, Iraq

"I do want to be Christian."

S., China

"I am surrounded by Muslims who will kill me if they find out that I pray prayers on your website and ask Jesus into my life. Please pray for me. I do not know a single Christian. You are my only contact."

Male, Afghanistan

"I was a Jehovah's witness. I had joined its cult and I am 20 years old—after listening to a preacher from the website godsolovestheworld.com, I decided to give my life to Christ, but my fear is that my life is in danger. They will try to kill me."

Male, Nigeria

"I was in tears reading your e-mail. First of all, I don't even know why you would want to continue corresponding with me, someone you do not know and who you only 'know' because I sent you an e-mail. But, your e-mails sound very genuine and you seem to really care. I found myself in tears where you were talking about the fact that God loved me. I just find that so hard to believe. In fact, I've had people tell me that God didn't love me, so to hear you so adamantly tell me that He does really baffles me. Isn't there a point in which a person could go so far that Jesus would not want anything to do with her?"

Woman College Student, USA

"I'm a new Christian and I want my whole family to believe and worship God, but they don't like it. They worship idols, and I don't like them worshiping idols and not God. But I have the right to believe in Him. My parents keep on warning me, "Do not convert into a Christian," and I don't know what to say—I just keep quiet. Please help me."

Young Woman, Africa

"My parish priest told me to check out your website in preparation for a meeting with him. I have been very troubled lately, bothered by impure and blasphemous thoughts. My fear was that I had committed the unpardonable sin—but last night I prayed the prayer on your website, and asked Jesus into my life."

Woman, USA

"I am Muslim but I want be Christian. I love the Christians—and I love Christianity, but my problem is that I am Iraqi and I escaped from Iraq to Syria from the Islamic terrorists. The Islamic terrorists killed my family and I got threats from them that if I return to Iraq they will kill me. I believe in Jesus because He came to me in my dream and He put His hand on my head. I have ask Jesus into my life."

S., Iraq

"Please pray for my emotional healing. My five-year-old daughter died a few weeks ago in a car accident. I was raising her alone. I have attempted to take my life two times these past weeks. I am in a care facility. I am not a Christian, but know God will hear your prayers on my behalf."

Young Woman, England

"I want God to be my personal Lord and Savior. I want God to take total control of my life. I want that my heart should be the Temple God."

Q., France

"I am a Hindu in India and I am very interested in knowing Jesus. However, I cannot give my life to Him because my parents have warned me they will kill me if I become a Christian. My life is in danger. Please help me. I am hoping Jesus will speak to me through you."

Young Man, India

"I have nothing to live for, so I thought about suicide and I wanted to just end my life. But I just could not do it because I knew that suicide is the only sin that is unforgivable. So please be honest with me, and please tell me if I am going to hell if I end my life."

Young Man, USA

"I love my Lord and I hope He accept me. Jesus Christ, I need you. I wish I can escape from my world and drop the 50 years I lived like as Muslim. I need you Jesus. I pray to receive Jesus for the first time."

Elderly Man, Afghanistan

"I want to thank you for helping me by your e-mail. That day I begged God for forgiveness and asked Him to have mercy on me. I felt forgiveness and felt purified, because of Jesus. Still, it was hard to believe that, after all I had done here on earth, He'd forgive me. Thank you again for bringing the faith in God back into my life. It is Him I need to follow, because I can't live without Him. I know now that it is only the Lord that can bring me everlasting peace, joy and love."

Young Woman, Vietnam

"Thanks for everything you have done. I was going to commit suicide, but this helped."

Young Woman, Latin America

"My name is Ervin and I do not remember exactly how I got your e-mail address, but God, knowing of my pain, guided me to Global Media in a time when I had hit rock-bottom, as they say. I had no hope, trusted no one, and I was going crazy, but my Lord's holy mercy saved me, because through you each week I would receive e-mails and they encouraged me to seek God and to try to live a righteous life. One step at a time I was slowly coming out of the darkness and into the light of my Lord. God helped me get out of all my problems. Thank you very much—you do not know how grateful I am for your help. When this servant was in need of help, God used you to make me see His mercy, kindness, forgiveness, patience, and LOVE."

Ervin

"Dear friends at Global Media Outreach, I want to thank God for leading me to know you. You have been a great inspiration to me, your messages have helped a lot by drawing me more and more closer to the Lord, and I am managing to deal with my weaknesses now in the way of God better than ever before. May the Lord give you all great peace and joy this Christmas and always, as you endeavor to be a blessing to many, many more!"

Anonymous

"To all staff in Global Media, may God Bless you all, and I want to thank you for helping me every time I need courage and advise, for every difficulties that I'm facing. I know only Jesus and God the Father is our life, Savior and true loving God. I'm working now in a war zone with no nice Internet connection here. Thanks again for helping many souls like me; please keep sending me messages. You're really a great help. May God bless all of you."

Anonymous

"Thank you Global Media Prayer for bringing me back to God. I'm going through some tough personal problems, and felt something was missing in my life. The load of my problems were hanging for too long. It's time to let them go, and let myself be guided by the One that created us—GOD!"

Anonymous

"How does one fully walk in and live in JESUS?"

Julius, Zambia

"I can't seem to find peace of mind. My sad past doesn't seem to want to let me look ahead to the future. I feel I don't know how to have faith or believe in anything or anyone."

Dave, USA

"I want to follow God with my whole heart, but I always give in to sin that is always fighting against my life. I really want to inherit the kingdom of God one day. What should I do to overcome this problem?"

Jackson, Namibia

"I've been feeling a void in my life, and haven't really been living my life in the ideal way. I want to give my life to The Lord because I'm tired of living my life the way I do. I'm taking everything for granted; I really haven't given thanks enough. I'm almost 24 years old, and have nothing to show for it. I don't have a job. My parents want nothing to do with me, and I really have nowhere to turn to. The "friends" I thought I could turn to have crossed me in the worst ways. I don't have any true friends anymore. It's just me out here, and I'm just finally realizing it. I want to change. I need to change. I need some type of help to change my life. Thank you—I appreciate you even taking the time out of your day to read this. You have no idea how much this means to me."

Amy, USA

"I closed my eyes, went deep into my heart, said I am sorry for all my sins, and I said I would like to serve my Lord. I need eternal life with the Lord in heaven."

Anonymous, Kenya

"I didn't think you'd respond back so fast. Thanks for under-standing (previously she had told me about struggles she'd been having with her parents and depression). It means a lot. And it's weird, because I don't know you, but I seem to find it easy to tell you things. And, well, I really don't know why, but until I e-mailed this to you—I was pretty much thinking about killing myself. I have no clue who you even are. But now I feel that somebody's finally trying to help me."

Young Girl, Kelowna, B.C.

"Well, I think the website is absolutely great because it is going to help in tremendous ways. All of the people who are searching for answers spiritually, or confused people who are searching for the truth—of which is why they are here."

Seventeen-year-old, California

"It's definitely very helpful and totally awesome just to have someone to talk to that I feel I can be totally honest with, and who in return understands how I feel and can really relate to what I'm going through. I love being able to just tell you what is on my mind, and that you can answer me honestly. It really helps."

Seventh-grade student, Indianapolis

"Thank you for guidance. As per your instructions I have accepted Jesus as Savior, I have just now prayed for Jesus to forgive my sins and I am ready to move forward as Christian (Eternal life)."

Nitin, India

"I forgot to say thank you for sending those websites to me. Well, thank you! Because now I can go out in the world and live like Christ did, and walk with the Holy Spirit within me every day."

Seventeen-year-old student, California

"I've been so depressed for so long. I found your webpage from an advertisement. I asked Jesus to be a part of my life and to help me become the person He wants me to be. I prayed with all my heart; I really, really, meant it. I can already feel Jesus making changes in myself. It feels wonderful. But, where do I go from here? I haven't been to church many times in my life. What church do I go to? What part of the Bible should I read? I really feel like Jesus wants me to go to church, to meet Christians and learn more about the Bible, but I don't know which one to go to. I hope you have some advice. Thanks so much for you help and your website. This is what I have needed for soooooo long!"

Anonymous

I can't tell you how much it meant to me when I received your message that you prayed for me and my family. I cried and had chill bumps knowing that someone who doesn't even know me cares about me."

Jenny

"I have learned something new today. Repentance is a change of mind! Thank you."

Anonymous, USA

"I just want to thank you for your encouragement and support when I was truly lost and sad. My life has improved. I was baptized and I have learned how to live outside my "comfort zone." I thank you so much. I had nowhere to turn and you were there for me. I want to do the same for others. Please tell me how to help in my own neighborhood. I went to the homeless shelter for Thanksgiving and I am involved in Operation Christmas Child, but I know I can do much more. You helped me and I want to help you. How can I?? Please let me know. Simple faith is very powerful. Thanks for showing me support. Now I can do the same for others!! Thank you and God bless you!"

Michelle

"I am so much encouraged by your website. Let me say that I have been going through a very hard time from being displaced because of the war in the Rift Valley province, being homeless, being out of school for a long time. Through all these, I have seen the faithfulness of God. Your website encourages me that though all may seem to fade away, Christ still loves me even more. That when I go to sleep without having supper, that is the time that God is seriously near me and taking good care of me. Though I am passing through thick and thin, God still knows me and cares for me. I am encouraged. Please remember me in your prayer, for God to have His way in my life."

Virginia, Nyahururu, Kenya

"I felt that I have never really belonged anywhere when it came to Christ. I have wanted to accept Him—I really have, but for some reason I could never keep up the commitment. I felt like I had betrayed my friends who kept taking me to Youth Group and church. The times I spent with God were fruitless. I need Christ in my life. I have been through many things in the past few years, and I am searching for some source of comfort . Thank you so much for helping me accept God. I feel at peace now."

Jade

"I've been clean for a month now, and it brings me to tears thinking about how happy I am that I've devoted my life to God. I'm getting 90s in most of my subjects—not drugs, liquor, no problems with authority. I feel like a new person, and I couldn't feel better because now I feel complete. I just wish my friends could understand, because I know that peer pressure is horrible. However, I've learned to deal with it, and say no. I just want to say that I think what you're doing is incredible. Staci's Story had me trembling with tears rolling down my cheeks. What an amazing person she was. It made me realize I want to leave my mark. I want people to realize who I stand for, and that's Jesus Christ, our Savior."

Kayla, Canada

"I beg your pardon at first because I really do not know what I should call you. I prayed as you taught me. I was very busy in these days because my son was ill and had an operation. I have some questions. As I said, I prayed but I do not know what else to do. Teach me, please. I am going to Tehran today to buy a Bible so I am very happy."

Touradj

"Your website has made a big impact on me. From reading y'all inspirational talks, it has helped me recommit to Christ and start becoming a better Christian. I have always been a Christian and a believer, but I believe that I was trying to be someone that I'm not. That is, someone that everyone else wanted to see. Your website helped me rediscover who I am. Also, the one part which talked about love made a huge impact, 'cause at the moment I'm going through a breakup. It showed me that Christ's love is the only true love I need. I WANTED TO THANK Y'ALL SO MUCH FOR Y'ALLS HELP! Keep up the work. If you're making an impact on my life, I know you are to others!"

Leslie, Houston, Texas

"Many of the articles on your website (M4M) are well written and rather profound. Although it was not this website that directly led to my prayer (just two hours ago) recommitting myself to Christ/God, I will continue to use your website as a resource."

Michael, New York

"Thank you for giving us strong hope and good wishes. The more we are getting from you, the more we are encouraged, and your giving to us is helping us grow in love and into strong Christians. I appreciate Global Media Group."

D., Sudan

"I have been following your website for some time, but today your "Weekly Prayer Focus & Responses" touches my heart. It looks like God is talking to me, but I still do not know what to do."

Anonymous

"Need prayers. Have NOT been with God for a long time. Want to turn back to Him. Will He forgive me? I feel ashamed even to pray and ask Him to. Will He listen to me? I'm in a desperate situation. Feeling soo empty. Please reply."

Malaysia

"I want to learn to read the Bible more often and to commit my life to Jesus Christ, for He has done mighty things for me."

Accra, Ghana

"I love reading the testimonies of others in Christ. I recommitted in July last year, and am always looking for information and encouragement to pursue my journey with the Lord."

Anonymous

"Sir, praise the Lord. I am Shwetha, doing engineering in my final year. I am born Hindu. My parents are completely against Christ. From the past three years I am into Christ secretly. I have many question. Can you please clarify them."

Shwetha, India

"I have given my life to Jesus, and ever since I made that decision my life has changed. Sometimes I get spiritual dryness, especially when I'm in a problem. What I normally do is use most of my time to pray, even though it takes time to get out of the situation. I would request you to continue praying for me."

Tanzania

"I've been trying to walk the right path, with our Lord. I have felt His presence before. I have issues in my life that sometimes keep me away from Him. I always try to make the right choice. I know I have a lot in my life. I want to feel the Lord's presence with me always."

Kentucky, USA (via text message)

"Thank You! I would like to become a better Christian. I feel like I am not the Christian I need to be. I just feel like I'm getting away from God. Please help me. I don't know what to do. I love God, and I know I'm a Christian—I'm just confused. Thank You!!!"

Maranda

"I have been a born-again Christian now for nine to ten months, but still I keep on sinning. I still do the old things I was doing, so please help me. What should I do so that I can be clean?"

Gift, Malawi

"Please, I want to know how do I really do the kind of things that Jesus Christ really expects from us Christians, and also how do I stay away from sin?"

Henry, Ghana

"I struggle daily, but I am growing in Christ. I need prayer for strength and making the right choices."

Tonya, USA

"I am in need of your prayer in order to grow in the grace of God and to be a man with full of God's anointing."

Mussie, Eritrea

"I believe in Jesus Christ, but have back slid and now need redemption and forgiveness in seeking my way back to the Lord. I love God, but due to my actions I wonder if God still loves me."

Brian, USA

"Does God really exist? If yes, why does He see us go through difficulties?"

Edith, Ghana

"Although I believe in Christ, I still have problems trying to understand why He would take my only son from me. My son was killed a few years ago and I still can't come to terms with it. I struggle with this every minute of every day. Please help me to understand this."

Melanie, USA

"I just have to say I was really touched by reading and going through your Four Steps to God, I was so emotional. Now I understand everything about Christ and why He died for my sins and that He loves me no matter how many times I have sinned, that He will still take me as His own child. And I'm very thankful for that. God bless!"

Kristine, Tonga

"I don't know what I want in life. Instead of making more money and enjoying pleasure, is there anything beyond wealth, power and fame? God please help me!"

Lim, Malaysia

"I don't know where to start. How do I accept Christ as the most important part of my life when I am going through such tough times and battling every day with loneliness and depression?"

L., Barbados

"How will I know that Christ is in my heart? I have prayed before wanting Him to come into my heart, but it didn't seem like it worked."

Brenda, Texas

"How do we know the Bible are the true words for God/ Jesus, and not things that have been changed over time through gossip?"

Rafael, Arkansas

"I am saved by the grace of God. But why do I have doubts? I feel as though I am not worthy enough to be that close to God. I have done bad things in my life and wonder, how could He forgive? I still continue to have bad thoughts that I know are wrong."

Teresa, Tennessee

"My name is Marina. I am from Mozambique, and I would like to tell you that I really find the Bible course very helpful and a good way for Bible consultation and to get closer to the Lord. I feel pity to submit the last one. Looking forward to carry on with the studies."

Marina, Mozambique

"I have enjoyed the Bible study very much, and it has helped me to grow more in the Lord and I hope you will continue to teach us more about how to live Godly lives, and this is what I want most."

Anonymous

"My name is Trang. Van is actually my little brother. I helped him send e-mails to you because he doesn't have an e-mail address. I witnessed to my brother when he received Jesus about a month ago. He is 12 years old and we live in Vietnam. (Me and my brother are believers, but our family are not.) I went on the Internet one day and found the website Godlovestheworld.com and thought all the messages were just right for my brother, a new member of our family, and he would need it. Thank you for helping him. Please pray for him that he will love God with all His heart, that His faith will be strengthened in Christ in spite of the persecution from our family. God bless you."

Trang, Vietnam

"Your weekly information has become a great source of enjoyment to me. I am a police inspector currently serving under African Union mission in Sudan–Darfur region where the place is 100% Muslim community. Through your program, I have an asset to the Word of God. May God richly bless you all."

Anonymous

"My name is Kelly from Kenya. I am 26 and am not saved. I have lived a live that I believe makes me feel unworthy to even say I am a son of God. What can I do? Is it possible to be joined with praying youths of age 26 or any prayer group? Jesus' death on the cross, in our place, paid for the penalty for our sins. What did we do for this penalty and how can our sins be forgiven through His death? Was there no other way but only through His death?"

Kelly, Kenya

"Thank you very much for giving me the opportunity to pray at 5:24 a.m. There is so much on my mind. I have lost my way with God and I want Him to be the center of my universe. Please pray for me and my daughter Dionara. She is 21 months old. Help me put Christ first in my life. Thank you from the bottom of my heart, God Bless you all."

Anonymous

"I was baptized a few years back and gave my life to Christ, but was weak to so many temptations after that and committed serious sins that I am ashamed and guilt-ridden. I have prayed for forgiveness but I just don't feel forgiven—I want to start my life over and be the person God wants me to be, but I don't know how."

South Africa

"A soldier may have to kill at will—how does one accept the consequences of his/her actions? And can one begin to ask for forgiveness?"

Miranda, Canada

"Why is it so hard for me to stop sinning? Why do I find myself doing what I would not love to do AND not doing what I think I should do? I seem to know the right things to do, BUT I kinda always do the opposite—I need help!"

Ugo, Nigeria

"My name is Alaa. I live in Syria. I am Moslem but I want be Christian. I love the Christians—and I love Christianity, but my problem is that I am Iraqi and I escaped from Iraq to Syria from the Islamic terrorists. The Islamic terrorists killed my family and I got threats from them that if I return to Iraq they will kill me. I believe in Jesus and I saw Him in my dream and He put His hand on my head. I hate the terror— and I hate the Islamic terrorists and I hate Islam, because of them I lost my country and I lost my family. I love the Christians because they love peace, but the Moslems love the blood. I ask Jesus to solve my problem."

Alaa, Syria

"I feel lost and have no direction. I feel lonely inside. I pray but I feel like I'm in a wilderness. Jesus Christ, I beg you to help me. All I want is inner peace and contentment—is it too much to ask for?"

Simone, Malta

"What is the deal here? How can we really talk to God? I am a Christian but have found myself questioning every- thing. Everything I have seen in church seems so unreal and irrelevant. I want to KNOW GOD. Help me."

Andy, South Carolina

"I've been praying for a year so that God would clear up all the mess in my life after my wife left me alone for no reason. Nothing happened, and I am still suffering great emotional pain. The least I could pray is to have more faith in God. But sometimes I feel that my faith in God is lacking. Why does God leave me alone suffering after praying to Him daily?"

Mario, Malta

"My desire now is to love and live a life for Him. But honestly, I have a problem in myself. Several times, I always feel uncomfortable with myself. I'm a shy introvert, and close. I look at others and I always feel that they're more lucky than me. They have something that I never have it. I always pray and hope to be changed and renewed by the Holy Spirit. But, can you tell me what shall I do to face this? How can I tell the love and truth to others if I'm still in this condition? Can an introvert be used with all their weaknesses? Help, Pray for me."

Female, Indonesia

"I have sinned in so many ways, and I really want you to help me plead with Jesus Christ for forgiveness of my sins. Am expecting your reply."

Mary, Nigeria

"I have backslidden. I gave my life in 1996 November 6, but I have fallen on rocky ground and find myself doing things I know are wrong, justifying my sin to myself. Help!"

Debbie, UK

"There are times where I really have faith in Jesus Christ and I always try my best to please Him. There are other times where I feel that I had lost the faith that I had before, and I no longer pray as I used to pray from before. I need help to know why such things really happen to me!?"

Diana, Saudi Arabia

"People all my life have told me that God has had a plan for me and my life. For many years I did believe in Him. But I can't seem to talk to God without yelling anymore. I am also sure that He has forgotten me, too. I stand alone in this world and the ones I did love are gone. I feel lost and lonely and it scares me to death. People have also told me there are angels all around us and that there are miracles every day. Well, I don't see them. People are killing and dying, stealing and lying, and people forgot how to love one another. So I guess my question is how can there be this wonderful God when so many things are wrong with the planet? Children and adults hurt and cry every day, and children are dying on our streets and some have nothing to eat. So can you help me find God in this horrible world? Because I see no reason to believe. Can you help me?"

Lisa Ann, PA

"I am trying to find my faith and believe that there is a God and eternal life when this life is over. I do not as yet wish to go to Church but I am reading the Bible every night. Is this enough to become a Christian?

Fiona, Ireland

"I'm a person who knows little about religion. However, I want to become a Christian. So please guide me how to become a Christian."

Jiuayan, China

"What a wonderful gift it is to come across your website this evening. I just did a search online. I searched "God with me." And you were the first (and only) site I clicked on. I love your explanations, your sincerity, and your truth. Thank you so much. I didn't want to stop exploring your site, but I have to get to bed. I'm looking forward to reading all you have to share. Thank you so much for your service. What a gift to others!!!"

Erin

"I made a mistake and had an abortion two years ago. It seemed like the easiest way out at the time. I have a seven-month-old little boy now. He is the most precious thing in my life, a wonderful gift from God. His smile and his eyes light up any room. I could not imagine life without Him, and such a horrible thing I've done. I have confessed my sins and receive Christ into my heart. Does He still love me and forgive me, for such an awful thing?"

Erica, MO

"I just want to have peace in my life, my family life, I need God's help. Help me, God."

Minushree, Amsterdam

"I thank God for your life. I went back from the Lord, but through your website I have recommitted my life to Christ. Again, I thought the Lord did not love me. I need your prayers to help me stand firm in the Lord."

Laura, Ghana

"I like Jesus Christ. But I am Hindu, from very different society. I don't know many things about Him. But when I hear about Him I really feel good. What does Accept Jesus mean? How can I accept Him, being Hindu? And how can I learn more about Him?"

Sarbani, Norway

"I am unable to understand the purpose of God in my life. I am in bitter spiritual crises, and need to know what the will of God is in my life."

John, India

"I know that God loves me and has done many things for me, but I realize that I'm not closer to Him. What do I do? I need your help to be back to Him, because I don't know where I'm going."

Chad, USA

"I was wonderfully blessed by your website, to which the Lord led me through a link in a LifeScript newsletter. I am a follower of Jesus, but have recently been battling a lot of personal issues and feeling pretty defeated. Your site helped me refocus on Christ after a very tough day. Thank you so much!"

Renee, Bavaria

"Please guide me—I do not feel the presence of God, but am trying very hard to connect with God in my way. Please show me how."

Tanya, GA

"I have been saved many years, and I backslid but came back to the Lord. This was a while back. I don't feel at peace, but that may be due to putting everything else ahead of God. I know what I should do, and yet I just skate along. I want the joy and peace I had. Can you help me?"

Nancy, North Carolina

"In recent times I have been struggling spiritually. But yesterday evening, I have been praying, thinking and working through that I need to be 100% for God, as many times I have been doing my own thing, going my own way and sitting on the fence, or lukewarm as in Revelation. I did pray to God myself and then also with my wife. Asking God to help me to repent, and also for His forgiveness. Also to allow myself to be 100% committed. To live a Spirit-filled life, with the Lord Jesus as Lord of my Life. So please pray for me that I will know God's power and strength over sin."

Peter, Australia

"I don't feel right. I am getting sicker every day. My family doesn't know what's wrong, nor do my doctors. Is God giving up on me, or is it me giving up? I will not go to church for my answers. What I really need to know, is God still there for me even if I had turned my back on Him before?"

Kenneth, Canada

"I'm 19 years old and call myself a Christian, but I am not as a strong a believer as I am supposed to be. I describe my relationship with Jesus as "ON and OFF" and I would really like to change to all this. I would love to receive Christ in my life internally, and grow to love Him even more."

Jacklin, New Zealand

"I want to accept Jesus Christ into my life. My life is nothing but turmoil, and I want to bring some direction to it.

Leigh, MO

"I would like to start a new life with Christ in it. I would like to set new goals in my life, and by God's grace, accomplish them."

Prosper, Canada

"I would like to receive Christ in my life. I am so tired of the way I am living, but I have faith and I know it will get better. I want to understand the word I read, but I do not understand. Please help me to understand."

Stephanie, MD

"I am in a very confusing, low point of my life right now. I am seeking help. I feel like my life is not going the right way it should go. I don't know how to pray. If I do pray, I feel like my mind is racing all over the place. People say—let it go! Give it to God! But how?"

Jelena, IL

"I can't go on the way I'm doing right now. I have many sins. That is the wall between me and Jesus. I keep on doing the same sins over and over again. I think God is tired of my repentance every time. He knows that I am going to do it again and again—I don't read the Bible anymore, neither do I pray. Please help me and ask God to help me, too."

Thea, South Africa

"I really wish I could meet the person that keeps sending me these wonderful e-mails. Just know this—you have brought me back to God and I thank you with all my heart."

Matt

"I am very happy to hear the Four Spiritual Laws. I would be very happy to know more about Jesus, because inside my heart I feel I want to get the word of Jesus Christ."

Amos, Tanzania

"I'm a Muslim, 22 years of age, from Pakistan. I don't know a lot about Christianity, but I believe that this is the true way and I believe that Lord Jesus Christ died on the cross for my sins, and He covered our body with His holy blood. I want to convert to Christian, and I need for help."

Waheed, Pakistan

"All my life I have lived as a sinner. I have now given my life to Christ, and our Lord Jesus has forgiven all my sins and washed me clean. All I want to do now is to live the rest of my life to our Lord and Savior who is Jesus Christ, the author and finisher of our faith."

Emekahre, Lagos

"I am a Christian, but my problem is that I just don't feel close to God right now, with all my problems piling up. I know that this would be the right time for me to talk to Him more often, but I don't. I'm feeling so weak in my soul. I feel so far away from Him. Can you help me? Please."

Allyna, Philippines

"I would like to know how to get closer to God and have that personal relationship. Please tell me how this can be accomplished."

Brenda, California

"I need your prayers to live, as I am in a lot of debts and cannot get out of it. Please also pray for my family members to come closer to Jesus. At the moment I have the tendency to commit suicide. Please advise me on what I should do to get out of this depression."

Cheryl, India

"It's refreshing to read about the Lord on the Internet, which is usually filled with pornography and filth. It was nice reading out of nowhere those words: God Loves You—in the middle of a page that talks about the war in Iraq."

Enrique, Mexico

"I have lost my husband recently in a tragic accident. I am unable to get over this loss; with the result, I have lost my faith in God and cannot accept the injustice that I am facing due to his death. Please help."

Corrine, India

"Hi. Sorry to ask this, and don't think I am being arrogant. If God was real, why are all of these problems in the world? (e.g., Africa, Third World problems, terrorism all among us.) There are so many problems and evil in this world, and I never see any sign of God at all helping. I am a very skeptical person and I believe there may be something out there. I believe a miracle did happen for the creation of everything, but is it science or God? I hope you will be able to give to me advice, and I hope if Jesus is true, He forgives my sins and lets me become a follower."

Scott, UK

"How can I feel Jesus in my life? How can I have peace in my life? I get too angry too much, and it's not good. I want Jesus to help me."

Rupali, India

"How do I know that God loves me?"

Yvonne, South Africa

"I have slipped and fallen back into the world ways. And I have also thought about suicide. So when I went on my computer, which I haven't done for a while, I am so glad I did. Thank you God for sending this e-mail."

Patricia, New Jersey

"I have felt very sad for the last decade. I don't have trust in myself and everything I try to accomplish. That's why I want to feel that Jesus is in my life. I need someone I feel I can trust."

Tanja, Netherlands

"I need help. I need to know how to pray, and I want to get to know God and Jesus. I would be glad if you could help me."

Miala, Canada

"How can I get closer with God? I've been asking for forgiveness, but I commit sins over and over again—so please help me to find the true happiness in life."

Mae, Philippines

"I want to learn more on how to live my life as God wants me to. I am weak and have much to learn. I need guidance so that my faith can become strong. Please help me."

Shirley, Canada

"I really liked finding this site on the web, because in these moments I feel I need God more than ever. I want to change many things about me that I know are wrong, and I wish I can do that and then help other people, but I don't know exactly how."

Alicia, Mexico

"I want Jesus to enter my life and to forgive my sins."

Joseph, Egypt

"I had been lost for long time. I have committed many sins. I want God to forgive me. Please help me know the name of Jesus."

Aghostino, Mozambique

"I am a Christian and I pray to God every night, but I can't understand this: Jesus loves us, right? So why are there wars and hunger in the world? Does He bring sickness on us? Does He want to punish us? I don't have an answer. Help . . . ."

Natalie, Malta

"This prayer helped me to be close to Him again. My faith was falling, and then I saw an ad and the ad said "Jesus Christ Loves You . . ." and so, thank you."

Lia, Vietnam

"I was actually browsing the Net to look for a job. Then I had clicked a website or link that led me to this website which is Global Media. Then I realized that it's been a while that I have forgotten Jesus Christ. Not to the extent that I have totally forgotten Him. What I meant to say is, sometimes, I forgot to pray or go to church. But somehow, I still manage to pray, but not like before when I was constantly and consistently praying everyday and going to church every Sunday. From this site, I realized that God is still with me. I have undergone a lot of trials and problems in life, but God made me feel that he's right behind me. He hasn't forsaken me, nor my family. This website is really helpful. As you can see, God is now on the Internet. Things have changed, like it really made me feel so light and blessed when I decided to give it all up to Jesus."

Anonymous

"I often face problems in my life, and I even feel that my family doesn't love me. I feel like a left out person in my family—my question is, does Jesus still love me??"

Vyna, Indonesia

"Hello dear brother. I am sending you my best wishes and greetings from the bottom of my heart. As you know, I was in a persecution situation, but today I met my uncle and some other men in the street. My uncle pointed his finger to me and told the other men that he is my uncle. My uncle was so angry and told me that I have spoiled the dignity of our clan. He also gave his last warning about my faith, and he told also me that he will kill me if I don't obey what his will, and I was informed that some of my clan people were meeting in our house recently and discussing about my faith and how I should come back to Islam. I am fearing for my dear life, so please pray for me and inform my situation to all the staff of your organization. Tell them also I need their prayers and say Hi to them. Your brother."

Muktar

"Brother, I want to say THANK YOU, THANK YOU for the messages of hope and of faith. I have received "faith," and no one in this world can take this away from me. I pray for you daily my brother, for I know that you are one of the Fishers of Men as indicated in the book of Matthew. I thank you my brother for the messages of hope "that Christ is coming again" and may God be with you."

Anonymous

I can't remember how I got to this website, but I thank God I did and I thank all the wonderful staff of Global Media Outreach. You guys really reached me. And how I came to Jesus, I was a bad reader and I needed to do so many things but I could not read. So one day a friend of mine said to me, "How well can you read?" I said not very well. We began working and I read best from the Bible, so that's how I know that Jesus is the way for me. And you guys show me that again, but I still need some more learning to do, so if there is any way you can help me I will love it. Keep sending me these mails and please help me."

Lindsay, Jamaica

"I've been a lip-service Christian for a long time, with a lot of doubt about whether I was actually saved. I'm not sure how I came across the Global Media Outreach website, but when I did, one of the headlines was "How Do You Know That You're Saved?" It caught my attention, because I still felt sinful and lost, though I claimed I knew Christ. I rededicated my life to Christ, and things have been very different then. Sinful urges I thought I'd always have to fight have gone away. I'm more optimistic about my life and my walk with God. I feel like I'm growing as a Christian again, which I haven't done in a very long time. Now I'm kinder; I'm not so cold to people. I don't feel like a hypocrite anymore. I feel like I can honestly talk to people I don't really know about Christ, and, what's more, I WANT to know. I'm not ashamed of my faith."

M., Oregon

"First of all, I was not a Christian. Now, since childhood I had a strong inclination towards Jesus. I don't know how; then in my childhood, I had no one to explain this as I started growing, I myself started looking out for things related to Jesus. Then I came across this website and now I have started reading the Bible. I get so peaceful when I pray to Him. I have prayers downloaded from the web and I have a strong desire to serve Jesus in church. I used to go to church, but now where I'm at present there isn't any church, but I say His prayer thrice or as many times. I pray and all my worries vanish away."

Female, Ghana

"Thank you for the gift of sharing via the Internet. I believe God gave someone the talent to write and use these programs to help us sinners as myself. Thank you for taking the time to share."

Rhonda, Texas

"I have struggled with my faith in God for many years. I would like someone to help me learn, believe and commit my life to God forever. Can you help me?"

Dale, Arizona

"I need and want a closer walk with God. I am drowning in my own mistakes. I need direction and the wisdom to make better decisions. I am so tired of making the same old mistakes, no matter how many times I pray for guidance I always seem to mess up. What is wrong with me?"

Lana, FL

"Before I repented, I was a girl who trusted in my own strength, intelligence, and my own power to solve my problem. One day, I got a big problem and realized that I was nothing, nobody could help me, and I realized the big sin I had done in my life. I started to ask myself whether Jesus still loved me or not, whether my sin could be forgiven, then I browsed Christian websites and tried to find the answer. You know, sometimes you can't talk your very tell private problems to your pastor, friends, or even your mum and dad. So I tried to find the answer in Christian sites. As I read how Jesus loved me and died for me, it was like a big thunder in daylight. It made me cry, and realized how I had wasted my life for nothing worthy; then I repented. I looked at life from a very different point of view. God created me for a purpose, now I'm sure. The purpose is to reach souls because God cares for souls as He cares for my soul and saves me. I spend my days by reading the Bible, outreach, have fellowship with Christian believers, pray for souls, in church, hallelujah. I saw all things as ridiculous before I repented, but now I like them all, praise the Lord. God must have changed the function of my brain."

Anonymous

"I want to be God's child, and I want to know about Jesus very much."

Lydia, India

"I have realized that God has done so much for me. He has been protecting me and blessing me with a lot of things. I love God with all my heart, and I want to know Him more than ever. My life is a mess right now without Him."

Naledzani, South Africa

"Thanks for helping me recognize the need for Christ in my life, especially during this time of so much problems in my life. I am a Liberian refugee living in Ghana as a result of the recently ended civil war, which claimed the lives of many of my relatives and burnt our family house down. This made it difficult to return at this time. I am now left with a brother and my fiancée and our three-year-old and seven-month-old daughters."

Mazu, Ghana

"I want to be more to God and Lord Jesus. I know sometimes unknowingly I get tempted to commit sins. Please help me. I am basically a Muslim and married to a Christian. I do rosary, attend mass, receive communion; but, I feel by doing all this I haven't still received Jesus in my life. I want to receive Him. Please help me."

Manifa, India (via text message)

"First of all, I would like to thank your team. You are doing a great job for the world—since I got born, again I observed that life is different when I compare the life that I was living before I was born again. I realized that being a Christian is nice and complete. My things were not going well before I knew Christ. Since I've received your inspired message of Christ, my faith has grown up, and actually I enjoy the reality of being a Christian—thanks for wishing to know about my life in Christ."

Foster, South Africa

"I have been receiving your messages for the past three weeks. I have learned a lot about how you can live a pure life to be closer to God. The messages I received have improved my Christian life, and have made me know how important it is to win souls for God. I thank God for your life and the wonderful work you are doing. Hoping to hear from you again."

Anonymous

"I just want to know about life after death. I lost my best friend and I am confused. I am afraid of death. What happens when a person dies?"

Namute, Tanzania

"I love the Lord, but lately I have lived in sin. I feel so lost; the peace and joy I have always had is gone. I need a lot of prayers."

Kalumba, Tanzania

"I feel unworthy of facing Him knowing that I have sinned. I don't want to send the Spirit away—but I feel as if that's what I'm doing when committing a sin. How do I handle it?"

Helene, Tanzania

"I'm a bit lost with my religion and beliefs. I'm only starting to understand the power and glory of God. Just more information is okay."

Warren, UK

"I've prayed for Jesus to come into my life—but there are still some challenges that are attacking me spiritually . . . . How can I change and leave them?"

Kasongo, Tanzania

"Thank you for giving me this chance, and directing me on how to seek forgiveness and accept Christ into my heart."

Chilala, Tanzania

"Thank you for giving me a way to make this decision."

Fadzai, South Africa

"Thank you for this chance to get back to the path of hope."

Charri, USA

"It is awesome that this is available to people on the cell phone Internet. This has truly blessed me and inspired my spirit."

Stacey, USA

"I once felt God's presence in my life, but I got lost along the way. I've sinned a lot ever since then, and I didn't even know how to approach anymore. What do I do?"

Julia, South Africa

"How can I fight the guilt of my former sins?"

Steve, Kenya

"Belief in Christ gives me a lot of piece of mind. To be forgiven is the ultimate reason to go on with life. I pray that the Lord Jesus will never forsake me."

Robert, Kenya

"Lord, let your glory spread across. It's wonderful to know about you Lord. Your preaching and teachings are so motivating. Lord, my life is changed. Thank you, Lord."

Mona, India (via text message)

"How do I get closer to Christ? My faith is so weak."

Carole, Cameroon

"My life was a mess, and having known Christ as a child, I realized that He was missing and that I had to find my way back to Him. He is all that I have ever needed. I was doing a google search on the name "Jesus"—now I have purpose and direction. I have eternal hope. I don't feel alone and messed up, or even out of order. I have regained my momentum and confidence. I have the knowledge that God is all that matters, and I now know who I am in Christ."

Anonymous

"I am very happy to let Jesus work in my life."

Minda, Indonesia

"I have now been serving God the Father for one year plus. In the one year, I stopped smoking, drinking and doing all the wrong stuff. I now realize that if God is with me, who can be against me? I have committed my life now in serving the Gospel of Christ. My destiny is before me."

Anonymous

"I've been converted to a Christian since two years ago; even though I thought I've left my old life, I still haven't received the power of the Holy Spirit over me. I still give up easily when things turn difficult in some areas of my life. What can I do?"

Angelica, Columbia

"I am a Hindu, but really interested and believe in Christianity. Can you help me?"

Greeshma, India (via text message)

"Thank you Lord for giving me an opportunity and moment to open me and accept You again. Thank You, Lord."

Ant, Philippines

"I love Jesus Christ and I will surrender my whole life to Him. And I want my family to receive Him."

Arlene, Philippines

"Jesus—I give my future for You . . . ."

Ester, Indonesia

"It's really great of you people to tell the world about God our Lord, and Jesus Christ, His son. I would love to do that, but I'm afraid that someone would not only make fun of me but hurt me like the stories in the Bible. Please help me. I love how you spoke strong words during the video and expressed clearly about the path of life. I have been a Christian for about all my life and I love every moment of it. I just chose for the faith response that I just prayed to receive Christ, because I have no idea what recommitted means. Sorry."

Daisy, Canada

"I'm keenly accepting that Jesus Christ, who is my Savior and gave my new life, He was crucified for me. I love Him so much, and I decided that I will live my life with Him."

Alliyia, Pakistan

"How do I know that the Lord Jesus is hearing my praying?"

Anneke, Netherlands

"I want to know Christ more and serve Him all the days of my life, but it's kind of difficult over here. I need Prayer 4 God to give me the strength, and also Prayed 4 Me on His favor all the days of my life."

Derrick, Belarus (via text message)

"I was checking some song lyrics on a lyrics website. Then I saw this advertisement saying "Jesus loves you," and I clicked that link because I wanted to be loved and will gladly join Christianity. I think my life really changed in some ways. After I became a Christian, I feel great, like I was reborn, and I feel happier than before. It feels like Jesus is always with me, and I am not alone anymore."

Anonymous

"How can I know/feel Jesus come to me?"

Nazirah, Malaysia

"Thank you for such a wonderful prayer, and the chance to accept Jesus as my personal Lord and Savoir."

Mylene, Philippines

"I am a Muslim, but I want Jesus to come into my life. What should I do? I would love to have my own Bible so that I can study the world of God. Is it possible to get one?"

Lyadi, Nigeria

"I love Jesus with all my heart, and I thank Him for the gift of life that He gave us."

Judith, Sweden

"I wish my family could understand Jesus as the giver of the eternal life."

Maphunye, Lesotho

"Pray for my son, so he should come near to the Lord Jesus Christ and that I may bear more fruits for His Kingdom."

Ranjan, India

"I often fail and fall in fulfilling my commitment. What can I do to keep on the "road" of committing my life to Jesus?"

Dience, Indonesia

"I want to know Jesus better and better, for I am not yet a Christian. I need to understand and have all my faith in Him, for me and my family to get closer to Him. Please help me."

Rajini, India

"I want to love Jesus without having any questions against Him, and I want to increase my faith in God. Also, I want the doubtful thoughts which rise inside me while I pray to vanish forever."

Desia, Nottingham, UK

"I pray that Lord Jesus would finally guide me in my life, so that I can understand and have a better point of view on how I must go on after so many years of being lost in lots of trouble, not knowing the way to choose, and His divine guidance so that I can still be with Him."

Yoga, Indonesia

"I thank you for this. I wanna commit myself to God again 'cause I've done many, so many things that was against the will of God. I want to repent."

Poppie, South Africa

"I love Christ very much, and I want Him to be my Savior."

Frederick, Ghana

"I've lived my whole life my way, and it's the wrong road. I truly want my soul cleansed to release my personal demons and truly forgive myself, for I cannot live like this anymore."

Craig, Ireland

"How do I find Jesus and let Him know I want to worship Him and praise Him? My family isn't Christian; but I believe in Jesus, but I can't go to church. What's an alternative until I'm old enough to go to church by myself?"

Lee, Saudi Arabia

"How would I know that I've received Jesus as my Savior? Because I've been praying the prayer several times but I don't feel anything. What should I do? I truly want to receive Him."

Chichi, Tanzania

"How can I stay with Christ forever?"

Jerome, Western Cape, South Africa

"How do I know if I am truly forgiven?"

Juanitta, Western Cape, South Africa

"I want Jesus always in my ways of living this life."

Segun, Nigeria

"Thank you for coming at a time when I needed you."

Andile, Swaziland

"I would love to serve God always."

Bongy, Gauteng, South Africa

"Jesus, i love u and i will live in you forever."

Deepak, India (via text message)

"I know God forgave me for my sins, but why do I keep falling back to the same sins when I don't want to?"

Tanya, Gauteng, South Africa

"I want to live my life clean, and want to forgive and put my entire life in the Father's hands."

Maureen; South Africa

"How do I strengthen the Holy Spirit in my life while my former sinful nature continues to control and rule over me?"

Niques, Kenya

"I feel bright already. I pray that I won't be easily swayed by temptations. Keep your good work up."

Festus, Kenya

"I want to serve the Lord with all that I have, and want to live for Him. I know the Lord. I just fell off for a while. But I want to serve and do His will. Please pray for my strength in the Lord."

Johnson, Ohio, USA

"I am very blessed to have recommitted my life to Christ, the Savior. Please pray for me and all my friends."

Ogwang, Uganda

"I want to live my life the way God intends for me to live it. Emotionally, I'm battling with my spirit. I need a change."

Candice, South Africa

"Please, I realize that I am falling away from Christ and am not doing what is good as a Christian. Kindly tell me what I should do to go back to Him. I am always angry with people around me for no just reason. What should I do to overcome these worries?"

Douglas, Lagos Nigeria (via text message)

"I'm a sinner. I need God to forgive me, and give me grace to follow Him to show others that Christ is the Savior of our soul. I will be happy to receive messages from you. Thank you."

Daniel, Abia State, Nigeria

"I wish to follow Jesus, and grow daily in His word."

Kathryn, Louisiana, USA

"I just need more courage to stay under His shadow, and defeat the devil every day of my life. I need His blessings forever more."

Georgina, South Africa

"Thank you soooooo much. I'm only 13 years old and just put Jesus in my life."

Delicia, Texas, USA

"I have realized that God has done so much for me. He has been protecting me and blessing me with a lot of things. I love God with all my heart, and I want Him now more than ever. My life is a mess right now without Him."

Naledzani, South Africa

"I backslid a few years ago. I have now rededicated my life with God. It seems like Satan is attacking me even more now. Please give me some advice in what to do. I need all the encouragement I can get."

Ivy, Washington, USA

"Thank you for such wonderful prayer, and the chance to accept Jesus as my personal Lord and Savior."

Mylene, Philippines

"How do you stay focused on the right way of life in this world that has so many negative people in it? How can I help spread the Word of God?"

Brenda, Indiana, USA

"I'm going through a lot of depression in my life from the things I have done in my past. I am asking for forgiveness and to give my life back to Jesus Christ."

India, California, USA

"I love Jesus with all my heart, but sometimes I do things that are wrong. What can I try to stop doing wrong things?"

Emmanuel, USA

"I know God forgave me for my sins, but why do I keep falling back to the same sins when I don't want to?"

Tanya, Gauteng, South Africa

"I want to live my life clean, and want to forgive and put my entire life in the Father's hands."

Maureen, Gauteng, South Africa

"Praise the Lord, Christ has changed my life so much and I am forever grateful."

Sam, Wisconsin, USA

"I've been having a lot of problems in my life, especially now with my marriage, and I've realized that I have to let God take control and trust Him with every aspect of my life. I'm glad that the Lord always gives us second chances. I plan on doing something good with mine. "

Amantha, Kentucky, USA (via text message)

"Today I had thought of Jesus in my heart deeply, but I never thought He would respond to me in this manner; i.e., through your website so miraculously. Thanks be to Him."

A., India

"I go round in circles with God because I have had severe rejection from people and Christians, and felt traumatized with my Dad coming and going over the years. I find it hard to know deep in my spirit that Father God sincerely truly loves me unconditionally, and will never leave me or forsake me. Please help me and love me, and e-mail me."

Joanna, Cornwall, UK

"I've been through a lot of difficulties in the past few months, but the Lord our Savior helps me to face it and accept all the things that I've been through. He holds me to having a new strength and He changes me to be more stronger. He loves me so my Faith in Him will be more stronger than ever. Our Lord and Savior is real and ALIVE. I experience His goodness and love for us."

Elizabeth, Japan

"Please pray for me, that as of this day I will live my life pleasing to God."

Denise, Jamaica

"I want to be closer to Jesus Christ more now than ever before. Pray for me to be a committed Disciple."

Aigbavboa, Lagos

"Praise God for giving me this opportunity to recommit my life to Him. I pray that this website will help to save more souls for our Lord Jesus Christ."

Nungsang, India

"I wish to serve Jesus for the rest of my life, and be filled with the Spirit of God."

Joseph, Nigeria

"Maybe God is guiding me to be recommitted to Him. It seems that I'm getting far away from Him."

Mharjie, United Arab Emirates

"I just want to know more about my Creator, God. So please, send any information which can help me to do so."

Tesfaye, Ethiopia

"Thank you. I have by faith received Christ as my Savior and Lord, and I am claiming the filling of the Holy Spirit so that through His Power, Christ can live His Life through me. I give Him the throne of my heart and complete control."

James, Maryland, USA

"Thank you very much for this page. I just discovered the Four Laws Of Spirituality. May the Lord God Almighty bless you."

Matias, Ethiopia

"I am a Christian struggling to stay committed to Christ. I need to strengthen my relationship with God."

Florence, Bedfordshire, UK

"I would like to open my heart to the Lord Jesus Christ and for him to be my Savior."

Wailein, Canada

"I am Buddhist, but in my life I got only help from Christian people and now I prayed to Christ."

Simul, Spain

"I would really love the almighty God to forgive me for all the sins I have committed. And I have accepted Jesus as my personal Savior."

Benjamin, Zambia

"I was Muslim and I have become Christian. I wish to tell every person in this earth that our Lord Christ Jesus is the Way and Life and Truth."

Saeed, India

"Thanks for the wonderful and great work of the Lord. I truly appreciate the spiritual encouragement. I shall be grateful for any other information to help in sharing the Word of God with others."

Stephen, Nigeria

"It feels so good to accept Jesus Christ as my Savior. I am not alone because He's always there to guide me."

Jacisse, Philippines

"I gave my life to Christ after the tragic loss of my son. I then drifted away, not attending church and doing what I wanted to do. I never really felt close to God, and am not sure if that is why I strayed. I need and want God in my life. The years following the loss of my son while living in Christ were the most content and peaceful years. I'm lost and need direction to get back to Him. Thank you for this website and your help in my search."

Christine, Illinois, USA

"I want any information you can send me. I want so much to grow to be a Christian."

Cheryl, Minnesota, USA

"I want to know more about Jesus Christ in order to strengthen my faith in Him, 'cause sometimes if I have a struggle, sometimes I forget that there is a God that guide us. That's all—thank you."

Jenelyn, Philippines

"I desire more and more to experience Jesus in my life. For this, what must I do?"

Llssy, India

"I am happy and I feel relieved and free. Thanks, and keep on the good work you have started."

Anthony, Nigeria

"The way in which the feelings were expressed gave a shock to me, and brought tears in my eyes."

Deepak, India

"I am so glad for the decision I just took."

Amaka, Nigeria

"I really, really want to follow God, but I need your prayers so that I can let go what I have to start to follow Him."

Petrona, Jamaica

"Thanks for the website. My family and I said the prayer together tonight."

Thomas, Indiana, USA

"Thank you for providing this opportunity and information on the Net. God should bless you."

Mercy, South Africa

"I am glad about my decision."

Kabejja, Uganda

"I want to know Christ more, and help me turn against my wicked ways."

Ryan, Uganda (via text message)

"I want Jesus to take each and every part of my life."

Benedicto, South Africa

"I need Jesus in my life A.S.A.P."

Johannes, South Africa

"This is what has been missing in my life."

Nthabi, South Africa

"Your website has helped a lot to change my life to Jesus my Lord and Savior."

Samuel, South Africa

"Please spread this all over to the world because many people don't know the real God."

S. Sasi, India

"Thanks for taking me back to Christ."

Kipkoech, Kenya

"This is a golden change by which we can meet Jesus."

Saagar, India

"Thank you for the advertisement. I have been wanting to receive Christ."

Phumlile, Swaziland

"I want to commend you guys for your good job. Well done! The Scripture has changed my life for the better. Thank you."

Ogundele, Nigeria (via text message)

"Thank you so much. I needed that so much—I feel as if I've been a dead man walking. I'm alone with my dog. Homeless; now, I don't feel so all alone. Thank you Jesus and our Father and you."

Robert, Texas, USA

"Thank you for the word of God."

Brian, Namibia

"Thanks for assisting me to give my life to Jesus Christ."

Siphelele, Gauteng, South Africa

"Thanks for your inspiration to change my life. Be blessed and kept in the Lord."

Lari, Kenya

"This website has changed my life—I've really appreciated it. I pray that God gives you more revelations to help people who are low in spirit like me. Thank you very much. Be blessed."

Peter, Tanzania (via text message)

"Hi there. I would like to find Jesus our Savior, and for Him to save me and to help me to have a better and a fulfilling life. I would like to follow His ways and to try not to be on the wrong path. Cheers."

U., Australia

"How do I go about telling others about Jesus? I mean, I have one or two non-Christian friends, and I really want to tell them about Christ but I do not know how or where to start."

A., India

"Does God hear the prayer of a sinner?"

E., Morocco

"I was not living my life for Jesus, so I just recommitted my life to Jesus right now and want to live my life as He wishes and do His will. It's hard. My mom is dying of cancer, and I don't wanna be alone."

M., Minnesota, USA

"I've done many wrong things in my life. I want to change my life, and ask forgiveness to my sins."

I., India

"I would like to thank you for this opportunity to recommit my life to Jesus; nowadays, it is more important to make friendship with God who created the world and everything. To say the fact, we need to bow down to the almighty God."

C., Malawi

"It's hard for me because I know that I have to go back to Him, but sometimes something always holds me back. I don't know what it is, but there's something always holding me back . . ."

F., Texas, USA

"I am bringing the Lord back into my life surely but slowly, and I thank Him for leading my way."

P., Canada

"I'm growing closer to Jesus each day, and want to continue to do so."

P., Idaho, USA

"Today I was born again with Christ. I am feeling God in my heart. I am a sinner, and ask God to forgive me for my sins. I receive Lord Jesus Christ, and want to follow His commands."

I., New York, USA

"I am a woman of God, and have accepted Him as the lover of my soul. I would love to grow in Spirit as a young Christian facing difficulties. I want to stand firm in Jesus' name. He is a part of me and I need to feel His presence every day."

A., South Africa

"I am feeling very lost and depressed. The only answer I think is finding Jesus and bringing Him into my life. I need this very much."

S., Grenada

"I backslid. I woke up realizing that a life without Christ is no life at all. Without Him, I am nothing."

L., Trinidad and Tobago

"Thank you for the information of Christ. I prayed the prayer of being one of God's children again. Pray for me so I can be strong in the Lord again."

M., Michigan, USA

"Thanks for reaching out. I miss God so much, and want Him back in my life for real!!"

E., California, USA

"I carry great sin and in shame to my Father. I have prayed to return to God, and leave all that is evil and sinful behind me."

N., New Jersey, USA

"I fell away from the Lord many years ago for really ridiculous reasons, and have now realized that He is the only One I really needed all those years. I don't want to lose any more time in serving Him, thanking Him, and making Him proud!"

C., Iowa, USA

"I feel so empty inside, and so alone. I don't want to feel like this anymore."

R., Canada

"I feel free inside again; praise God."

L., California, USA

"The Lord is our Savior, and so I recognize this deeply in my heart."

M., Venezuela

"I tasted the miracle of Jesus Christ, and I want to accept Him as my Savior."

S., India

"Thank you for the prayer; I think it will change my life."

S., South Africa

"I am ready to change from my bad ways."

M., Nigeria

"Jesus, save me from misery, and give me the power to forgive."

M., India

"I really want to change my life. I have been through a rough time now, but I still believe in my Lord Jesus and want to go further to get to know Him better because I know He has a plan for my life."

N., South Africa

"I have started going to church, and want Jesus in my life. I want to change the way I live my life and live for Jesus. I ask the same for my children."

B., Florida, USA

"I want to grow deeply in the love of Christ, and to recognize Him as my only Lord and Savior."

N., Cameroon

"Thank you for this website. I want a closer walk with Jesus, and truly need Him every second of the day."

D., Washington, DC

"Jesus saved me from death, and I gave all my life to Him."

M., Ghana

"Truly, I do believe that Jesus is Lord and He died for my sins. I accepted Him to be my Savior."

H., Tanzania

"I am so thankful that our Lord is so forgiving and just. Thank you, Jesus."

J., New Hampshire, USA

"I surrender my life to Jesus. Please do help me pray, and for my whole clan to always have faith in Christ Jesus despite all the difficulties that the world offers. Thanks."

Michelle, Philippines

"I have been out of work for four months due to surgery. I am a nurse on an Alzheimer's unit. During my time off I have renewed my faith in God, and have begun the most wonderful spiritual journey of my life. I thank God every day, and ask Him to keep me in the palm of His hand as I now know He has always done that. I just have been awakened to His most holy presence."

Colleen, Tennessee, USA

"I am in a storm in my life at the moment, but I believe God will get me through it!"

Tom, Ohio, USA

"That was a really good little video! I liked it a lot; and I had been thinking about my faith all day when I saw this, so it must be a sign. Thank you."

Astrid, Norway

"I need more of Him in my life."

Ferdinand, Nigeria

"I really do recommit myself to the Lord to be my Savior!"

Chokaveti, Fiji

"I need Jesus in my life. I cannot function without Him. He is my source of strength, my Savior and my true friend."

Keitumetse, South Africa

"I have lost my faith for close to four years, and I want to recommit my life and self to God."

Fabian, Mongolia

"I'm wondering if Jesus Christ still loves me, despite of all my sins?"

Gina, Philippines

"At last, someone made a page for people to receive God in their lives. THANK YOU whoever you are. God gave me this gift today to enter your website. Thank you very much, God."

Christian, Guatemala

"It's really a very nice experience knowing Jesus Christ. All that I want is to grow in Him in all aspects of life; and to serve Him, as well."

Matovu, Uganda

"Thank you for sending me this letter. I really need Jesus Christ in my life because my life is in trouble."

Marian, Philippines

"Thank you for taking your time to help me to continue to grow as a Christian. I know that it won't always be easy, but God will be with me through it all!"

B., West Virginia, USA

"I need to get the Lord into my life, so I can become a better person and to receive Christ into my life. Yes, I need Him in my life so I can stop the thing that I do wrong. I am a little weak in some things. I need to get strong."

W., New York, USA

"This is a pleasure, and a chance to get to know more about Him."

M., Philippines

"I would like to change my life around, but sometimes I just don't know how. I do believe in my Lord, and with everything that I've been through, no one can ever take that away from me."

B., Arkansas, USA

"I thank you for giving me this opportunity to get close to God."

E., Italy

"Thank you for this website, so that I can grow my walk with Him."

A., Philippines (via text message)

"Thanks for being so helpful and kind, and sharing Jesus with me. I'll be very thankful to you for this."

S., Pakistan

"I have sinned a lot, and I just want God to forgive me. Now I've recommitted my life to Christ."

J., Fiji

"I want to know all about Jesus Christ, and I want to believe in Jesus Christ and to be happy with my life."

U., Mongolia

"I love Christ, and I want to serve Him all my life."

R., Rwanda

"I acknowledge that the Lord is my God, the one and only. I give Him my heart and soul just to be close to Him."

A., Seychelles

"I need God so much right now in my life to help me and help me to find my way back, 'cause I'm totally lost."

N., Seychcelles

"I really appreciate this online gospel."

T., Nigeria

"Thank you very much! I needed to be reminded that I'm not alone—there is someone always watching over me. Thank you, may God bless you."

T., Norway (via text message)

"It's nice having things like this because it helped rebuilding our relationship with God."

S., Nigeria

"I was checking for the weather here in Indiana on my phone, and this was above the forecast! Wow! I needed to see that!!"

K., Indiana, USA (via test message)

"I would like to learn more about this Jesus."

C., Tanzania

"Thank you for building this website."

D., Australia

"I prayed this prayer, and it's wonderful. I can feel Christ inside of me."

B., Jamaica

"I want Jesus to work in my life."

K., Tanzania

"Happy to be born again."

K., Kenya

"Thank you very much for having such a website. I believe it will help more people. May the Almighty God bless you abundantly."

P., Kenya (via text message)

"I just want God to take control of my whole life."

M., South Africa

"This is just what I have always wanted to find on the Net. I need more of such encouraging info!"

L., Tanzania

"I thank God as I clicked to this website. I really enjoyed the preaching, and I will be committed to Jesus for the rest of my life."

T., Slovakia

"It's AWESOME to have something like this on the Internet."

B., Western Cape

"Thank you for this website—it will help me grow spiritual."

A., Gauteng

"I don't want to sin no more. I want to follow Jesus Lord God Christ forever and ever. Thank you very much."

K., Guyana

"I just want Jesus to come into my life and to be my Savior. God bless."

I., Nigeria

"I've done lots of bad stuff in my life. How do I redeem myself in my mistakes?"

N., USA

"I have become closer to Christ in the last few weeks, and I feel a lot happier. I wish I had done it long before now."

R., South Africa

"First time to know God—still be learning."

C., China

"Am happy to find out about this website today. I pray that God will see me through in all my endeavors, and to give me strength to run heavenly race. What can I do to avoid sin?"

T., Nigeria

"I thank God for saving me. I hope to receive more information about growing in God's kingdom."

K., Nigeria

"I believe in Jesus Christ—He has touched my life in so many ways. I just want to keep growing in His love and mercy."

M., Maryland, USA

"I want Christ to take control of my life."

M., Liberia

"I have given my life to God years ago, but I have been falling short 'cause I have been letting things around me bring me down, but I thank God for me running into this site now. I am a new person in Christ; I can move forward now. I thank God for you all. I know this is God's doing—He knows just what His people need."

L., Florida, USA

"I love Jesus Christ and I receive Him. I want to live with Jesus forever, so I want to learn about Jesus Christ in detail and to receive the Holy Spirit."

S., Greece

"Can God forgive you if you have repeated a sin more than twice? I have gone to confess my sins, but do not understand how terrible sins can be forgiven."

G., UK

"I was foolish and almost murdered last week. I have had some close calls in my life lately. I want to accept Jesus as my Savior. I want to be happy again."

R., North Carolina, USA

"I want to repent all my sins committed to God, and renew my whole life."

M., Italy

"I was feeling sad this evening while doing my homework. Finding this website accidentally had lifted my soul and reminded me of the faith I have in God. God bless you for your efforts. Can I get regular leaflets or e-mails about God?"

H., UK

"I feel that I truly need God in my life. This prayer has helped me to gain that confidence in Him. Knowing that He will save me and keep me free, and help me through my youthful life and reassure me that God will be there whenever I need Him; and for whatever, even if I have sinned, He will forgive and keep me."

F., Belize

"This website was a beautiful refresher for me, and made me realize even more how important God is to me and how much I truly love Him—thank you."

A., New York, USA

"I have wanted to get my life in order and receive Christ for a long time. When this came up, I saw it as a sign. I have gone to church my whole life and never really received Christ—now, I have at home."

S., Georgia, USA

"I was always feeling like I am lost. Sometimes I think about death, but now I am a new creation."

M., South Africa

"Does God really listen to my prayers? Does He still have the time for me? There are so many people in the world for Him to have time for me, and to think I've been a bad child—but I want to change, and be a child of God."

J., Philippines

"I want to thank you for having this website available. I'm going through some things right now, and I know I can't get through them but with Christ by my side."

M., Georgia, USA

"Will He accept me still, despite my faults and failures?"

T., Philippines

"How do I know Christ has accepted me back from my sins?"

A., Ghana

"Am I worthy to share Jesus with others, despite of my sinfulness?"

T., Philippines

"After visiting your website, I will like to have further information on Jesus and the Christian doctrine."

F., Ghana

"I want to turn my life toward Christ."

B., Bengal, India

"I want to know about Christ."

P., Myanmar

"I am a man who wants the Lord to guide and teach me. I am a sinner, and sometimes weak. I need God's healing and strengthening power now more than ever. Please say a prayer for me. Thank you."

F., Columbia

"Thank you. This website was very profound in displaying the points of becoming a Christian."

L., UK

"I am so grateful to you. I did not know about your website until a friend sent me one of your e-mails! Ever since then, I live a better life because of the rich messages. Thank you very much."

M., Uganda

"Basically I am of the Hindu origin, but from my childhood I have a strong desire to know who is the real God, and I began to search. Finally I found the real God. No, no, only He shows me the way to find Him. Now I have a strong belief in Him."

L., Andhra Pradesh, India

"What can I do to stay with Christ all my life? I want Him to be with me."

K., Rwanda

"Thanks for this special program."

L., Malaysia

"I want to know about God. How God can help us. I am Hindu. But I want to know about Christian religion."

K., Haryana, India

"I'm emotionally damaged. I strongly needed Christ to lead my life. I need Him to restore and give me strength, to face the challenges of life as a new man. I pray that He will help me to bring my family back together and restore my broken marriage. I truly accept Him as my Savior."

L., Gauteng

"I want spiritual encouragement. How I can understand the Bible and get to know God's will over my life?"

D., Kenya

"I have received Him at the age of 16, but was not working for Him or knowing Him. But now I know Him, and I work under Him."

T., South Africa

"I accept Christ as my Savior."

J., Ghana

"I truly believe that our Almighty One is in my life. He is our Savior and the Father of all people in the whole universe."

S., Puerto Rico

"JUST beginning to change my life, and going to have a much serious and deeper relationship with God through His Son Lord Jesus Christ."

E., Fiji

"I want to be born again. And know how to receive Christ as my personal Savior in the Lord."

G., Ghana

"I and my family want to make it to Heaven in Jesus' name."

O., Germany

"I just want Jesus Christ to be more renewed in my life. I want to be more focused on Jesus Christ like never before."

K., Nigeria

"I wanna commit myself totally to God's will all the days of my life. I need guidelines."

A., Nigeria

"I would like you to pray for me so that God holds me strong. Thank you!"

M., Rwanda

"Thank you for helping me get back to God. I need materials to help me grow in God. Thanks."

D., Nigeria

"Thanks for this wonderful website. I am happy to recommit myself to my Crucified Christ. May God bless Global Media Outreach ministry abundantly to preach and share His Glory (the Crucified Christ) to all nations."

M., Indonesia

"I know the truth, but why is it that I chose to live in a lie? I love God, but why do I chose to live in the pleasures in this world?"

J., Philippines

"How do we know if the decisions we make are in God's will?"

T., Philippines

"I acknowledge Him as my Lord and personal Savior."

O., Nigeria

"It is true that God really loves us?"

M., Philippines

"Can a Muslim turn Christian? Muslims have just one solution to this problem—kill the man and his family, and I don't want to die."

M., Pakistan

"I am happy I visited this website. I need Lord Jesus in my life more than anyone else."

C., Tamil Nadu, India

"Can you please help me to grow my commitment to Christ and my faith in Him?"

Z., South Africa

"I know God is always with me, but how do I overcome the difficulties of this world?"

H., Zambia

"What must I do to be more dedicated to the things of God daily?"

I., Nigeria

"What can I do to know Jesus Christ correctly?"

R., Benin

"I pray God to help me follow Jesus Christ's path of righteousness."

I., Tanzania

"I have a desire to know God more, and to know how to live with Him through the rest of my life."

S., Ethiopia

"I commit my life to Christ who strengthens me when am really down, discouraged, heartbroken, and in trials."

E., Dubai

"I need God's intervention in my life."

E., Cote d'Ivoire

"I want to grow more."

D., Karnatka, India

"I believe Christ died for our sins, and through Christ we find love."

K., Botswana

"I believe that Lord Jesus Christ is the only Lord who has power to forgive my sin. In India, it is too difficult to receive Him as personal Savior. After carefully study, I have decided to commit my life for the Christ."

P., Orissa, India

"I have found it very difficult in recent months, but I have put my faith back in Christ to help me through things with the power of prayer."

E., UK

"How can I receive the Holy Spirit?"

P., Philippines

"Lord Jesus is my Savior. I love Him."

A., Maharashtra, India

"From today I believe in Jesus as my Savior! Amen."

R., Malaysia

"I'm actually born again. I discovered your website by chance. I would like to grow more in Christ, and gain more knowledge of the word so that I may help and introduce more people to Christ."

M., UK

"I would like to grow up in my spiritual life to love God more than I do now."

J., Timor Lorosae

"I have a lot of sins, and I want to change."

R., Alberta, Canada

"I just want the Lord in my heart. I want the Lord to dwell in me."

M., Zimbabwe

"Thanks for bringing me closer to Jesus Christ."

T., Liberia

"I've been longing to receive newsletters or letters about topics like this."

G., USA

"I want Christ to change my life anytime."

L., Indonesia

"Can my past sins be forgiven? If yes, then please pray for me to forgive my sins that I have committed."

S., Chattisgarhh, India

"I would like to understand the Bible, and to be shown how it can influence my life. Thanks, Debbie."

Debbie, UK

"Please pray for me to go back to God."

J., Philippines

"These past days I felt that as if I'm running away from Christ. That's why I want to recommit myself to Christ."

N., Philippines

"I need Jesus to come into my life and be the head of my family. I love Him so much that I can never do without Him."

C., Cote d'Ivoire

"I've accepted Jesus as my personal Lord and Savior."

I., Nigeria

"Need serious prayer so that I don't backslide as a former Muslim."

A., Nigeria

"It was about time I turned back and acknowledged what He has done for me. I want to draw so much more closer to Him as a child."

F., South Africa

"How can I really live my life with offending God, or abusing the perfect sacrifice that His only begotten Son paid on the cross for my sins and the sins of all men?"

E., Liberia

"God is good!! Hope that everyone on earth will have this opportunity to know and receive Christ Jesus to be their Savior."

W., Malaysia

"I want to know how to behave as a Christian? The character of a Christian??"

B., Western Cape

"How can a person who had believed in God then walked away be sure that God is happy that He is back. Is God going to take me serious?"

S., Kenya

"I love Jesus very much."

D., Indonesia

"I have accepted Jesus into my life, and would like to serve Him for the rest of my life."

P., Zimbabwe

"I want God to forgive me my sins and welcome me back to His side, for I have gone astray because of frustration. I have no one to help me both financially and otherwise, but I believe that God will favor me this time around. For He said I should cast all my burden on Him for He beareth it."

P., Nigeria

"I thank God for driving me to this website today!!! I have absolute belief that my life is going to change as I prosper in the word, due to this site!!!"

T., Botswana

"I want a sanctified life."

W., Botswana

"I want to follow in Jesus' footsteps, and give myself to God."

R., Namibia

"Is the prayer true? Because I have many problems in my life."

A., Mauritius

"I prayed for something on my phone from the Lord just today. Thank you."

L., California, USA

"How can God see my heart?"

S., Cambodia

"I'm a sinner looking for a Savior."

J., Egypt

"I believe in Jesus."

R., Brunei Darussalam

"I thank God to let me remember through this short message you have given me."

A., Tanzania

"I am a believer but have a lot of set backs."

C, Guyana

"What can I do to keep strong in Jesus?"

K., Jamaica

"You just got me at the right time."

M., Beau Vallon (via text message)

"I want to serve the Lord with all my heart."

S., Togo

"I want to grow further spiritually. How do I help myself?"

Z., Swaziland

"I really need God in my life. Thank you for opening my eyes."

M., Namibia

"It is my prayer to be closer to Christ."

A., Macao

"Need to grow spiritually; I'm not where I want to be and I'm sinning too much."

N., Gauteng

"I was looking for something else on my phone. I got another. God truly works in mysterious ways."

M., Kenya

"I love Jesus and I want to be with Jesus forever. But my mind finds joy in sins. I think I need a good confession. I want to remove all my sins forever. I know I want Jesus, not sins. How I clear from my sins?"

C., Sri Lanka

"Thanks for bringing a Christian program to the Net. I am lucky to have found you, and I want to receive Christ."

M., Nigeria

"Lord, I believe in you."

W., China

"I've lived this life of sin, and just want to turn back to God. I've lived the life of a gay man the last few years. And I believe that this is not what God had planned for me. Please pray with me and help me to turn from my wicked ways."

M., Gauteng

"Thanks for changing my life."

J., Kenya

"You found me at the nick of time."

W., Kenya

"I want to believe more, accept more, love more, and know more about Jesus."

I., Philippines

"Thanks for your prayers and encouragements in Christ. Question—what are steps to conquer fear and temptations in daily life?"

J., Kenya

"I'm a born again child who need to grow spiritually."

L., Gauteng

"I want the Lord to come to my life forever."

S., Ghana

"I want to know Jesus more, and I want God to forgive me all sin."

A., Norway

"Can Jesus use me to work for Him?"

L., Monaco

"Thanks for leading me to Christ."

B., Ghana

"I feel relieved and free right now. Hope this feeling never leaves me."

A., Norway

"Thanks for reaching out to me with the greatest gift ever."

B., Nigeria

"I cannot go through life without Jesus in my life."

L., Norway

"I need my lifestyle to change."

J., Guyana

"I want know more about God."

I., Nigeria

"I am looking for inner peace."

N., Kenya

"Please help me to know Jesus better and grow."

E., Kenya

"How can I grow in the Lord?"

S., Swaziland

"This prayer did a lot in my life and I want to say thank you."

C., Guyana

"What shall I do to completely be saved?"

J., Tanzania

"I want Christ in my life always."

A., Monaco

"How sure can I be that my sins are forgiven?"

T., Gauteng

"How can I be saved?"

C., Namibia

"Thanks for the words of encouragement from your site."

D., Kenya

"This prayer and its words help you realize that God gave His life for us; and well, we make mistakes, but God is the only one that can judge anyone."

P., California, USA

"I am a sinner and needs the Savior. HELP."

M., Gauteng

"Will Lord forgive my sins?"

R., India

"How can I learn to trust God?"

J., Tanzania

"Thanks for this. I want to pray God for a triumphant life over sin and temptation."

W., Gauteng

"It's a blessing to have this new website for the Lord."

E., India

"I was a Moslem. My sister was the one who encourages much to accept Jesus."

A., Tanzania

"Dear brother, thank you for this wonderful prayer. I love Jesus because He is my Savior. No one can save me, only Jesus. Praise the Lord."

I., Uganda

"How I can feel Jesus with me and help me?"

E., Egypt

"I thank God for helping me know this website, and making me to understand that He loves me more than I love myself. I am very happy tonight—in fact, the most wonderful night of my life. I hope He will never fail me 'cause I am passing through the toughest time of my life right now. I pray He will never fail me."

E., Nigeria

"I closed my eyes, went deep into my heart, and said I am sorry for all my sins; and I said I would like to serve my Lord. I need an eternal life with Lord in Heaven."

S., Kerala, India

"I tried to do what was right and required of me, by God but I always let the devil steer me away. I got into some serious trouble with the law and it changed my life forever, even though I still have a way to go with the trouble I got into. I have faith in God, and I know God will take care of me."

L., Louisiana, USA

"I just recommitted my life to Christ, and it has changed my life completely."

J., Maryland, USA

"Hi, I was just going over things when I saw this ad and read it, and thought for a second that I better recommit my life to Jesus Christ again since it's been years that I been in the world. I really want to change my life, and maybe you could send me some reading material. Thank you dearly, and may God bless this ministry."

O., El Salvador

"Thank you for making Jesus much near to me . . . ."

M., Philippines

"I'm a Christian, and I thank you for making a website like this. It helps me share my faith with my friends. Continue serving God. God bless us all!!"

J., Philippines

"I'm happy to recommit my life to Christ, and I hope you will help me. Thank you."

R., Ghana

"Thank you very much for allowing me the opportunity to recommit my life to Jesus Christ. I now have joy in my heart. God bless you."

A., Zimbabwe

"Thank you for your kindness of helping people, especially someone like me who can easily give up. Need the Lord's presence in my life and in my family. I'm sure with your help, all will be well. Be blessed."

E., Zimbabwe

"Just like to thank you all for the prayer. It really touched my heart."

L., Bulgaria

"I am an Indian Hindu girl. I have been directed to this path by a spiritual person who is a Christian. After accepting Jesus into my life, I am feeling that He is protecting me, caring for me and is beside me always. My own father hates me, and has driven my mother out of the house for another woman. Both my father and the woman try to create as much problems as they could in my life. Even that woman is now trying to break my marriage by inciting my father against me and my in-laws. So please pray for me, so that God foils their evil plans. Praise the Lord!"

S., Orissa, India

"I already accepted Jesus as my wonderful Savior, but I want to know more about Him. And I want to give some to others as well, so I would like to have His material from you."

D., Nepal

"I am so very grateful because I know that He that called me is faithful to carry me through. God bless you for caring for souls outside your vicinity."

I., Nigeria

"How can I commit myself to Christ? How can I be with Christ in the world?"

M., Lagos

"I need God's intervention in my life."

J., Guinea

"I have decided to follow Jesus now, and forever."

F., Indonesia

"I need the Lord in my life, and need a completely changed life in salvation. I am committed to Christ, but I keep backsliding. I pray the Lord keeps His hand on my life and controls it."

P., Uganda

"What must I do to expect Christ in my life? I really want to be a child of God, just the way I should be."

K., Dominica

"How can I maintain my conviction when I live in a communist nation?"

F., Vietnam

"I love Christ, and give my life to Him."

J., Sudan

"I want to grow, but don't know how."

M., China

"I'm really desperate for Christ. Please send me some information to help grow my faith for Christ."

R., Papua New Guinea

"I want to be used for God's work and the purpose for which I have been chosen. I have submitted my life to God and I want to be used for His glory."

B., India

"I am ready to know about Christ."

T., Ethiopia

"I live and work in a country where Christianity does not exist, but have been raised by my parents who are staunch Christians in Kenya, so I appreciate you sharing much. God bless you mightily."

M., Saudi Arabia

"I want Christ in my life as my Savior"

S., Cote d'Ivoire

"It's good that there's word of Christ spreading in the Net."

A., Poland

"I really like God. I need and love Jesus."

A., Tanzania

"I know the way that God worked in my life to save me from the most dangerous and reckless person I know. Myself. I believe that everybody should know about how wonderful Jesus Christ is. If He could forgive my sins, then He will surely forgive everyone else. All they need do is ask and be sincere."

G., Limpopo, South Africa

"Does God forgive our everyday sins, no matter how small we may think they are?"

S., Zimbabwe

"I've only just started going to church and wish I had gone a long time ago. It's the best thing that has ever happened to me, and the Lord has touched me in so many ways. We have a wonderful pastor and he is baptizing me this fall, and the Lord will be with me always. Thank you, Lord."

J., Manchester, UK

"After this prayer and during it, I felt this good thing in my heart and it felt good—like something touched me."

A., California, USA

"Thank you very much. I was going on a destructive path and I saw this prayer, 'GOD DOES CARE FOR US.' I thank God who wants me to be sinless, and for helping me whenever I go astray, and still helping me for what I am today. I owe my life to Him. It's really a wonderful feeling that there is someone for you always to forgive and accept you, no matter how bad I was. THANK YOU LORD. I praise you all my life. Please be with me. Guide me and help me all along the way till I reach you. I love you."

A., Goa, India

"I need to get to a better life. The one I'm leading is KILLING me."

C., North Carolina, USA

"Though being a non-Christian, I believe in Christ and I want to know more about Christianity."

A., India

"Praise the Lord!!! Life is wonderful with Jesus. I hope and pray that God will give me strength to continually and unselfishly provide a time and effort for enriching my faith to please and love God. I would want to grow as a Christian."

G., Philippines

"I really want to be good and devoted Christian. And I want to do that with the help of good and true Christians. Thanks for this wonderful opportunity to follow. May the grace of our Lord Jesus Christ be with you all."

N., Nigeria

"I want to give my life back to the Lord Jesus because He is so wonderful. I am going through spiritual warfare for the many mistakes that I have made in my life. I am depressed because I don't know how to move on. I stepped out of God's way because I was looking for love in all the wrong places. I don't know how to move on due to my bad decisions. I wish I had someone to talk to: a true friend."

J., Florida, USA

"Wow! I don't know what to say, but God is giving me the words to speak this, right now as we speak. God was giving me the exact feeling as stated in the article that taught me how to pray better. I was amazed at how God made me burst into tears as I realized His amazing untouchable love for me! And that He does care for me. And that He has been longing for me to open up to Him like a kid who misses their parents deeply or how a parent longs for their child when their child isn't theirs. The article I read has forever impacted and changed my outlook on life in the most amazing way. I thank God for giving me this prayer through your website—have a wonderful day, and God Bless you."

D., California, USA

"I want to have Christ in me."

B., Nigeria

"Please help me with my problems. I always want to read the Bible. Whenever I try to read it, something would distract me and I would forget to read. Also, I could never concentrate in my prayer. Whenever I close my eyes and pray, I would fall asleep or my mind will diverted somewhere else. I don know why this is happening to me. I wanted to pray and read the Bible from my heart. Please show me the ways to become a better Christian."

M., Meghalaya, India

"Thank you for the wonderful website to help sinners back on the road to Christ. God bless you!!"

T., South Africa

"I have not been to mass or been in church for over 26 years. I've always been kind of mad with the church and God. I guess my question is, 'does God forgive 26 years of pure sin?'"

D., Florida (USA)

"I want forgiveness for all my mistakes in life."

M., Philippines

"I have been doing a Bible study with my sisters for the past months, and have learned a lot and need to always learn more to keep growing spiritually and understand all I can about the word of God and Jesus the Son of God who is our way to eternal life."

J., Florida, USA

"God came and transformed my life."

B., Congo

"I want to be closer to God, and to give back the love that He gave to me. I love God because He is my Savior and my best friend."

S., Philippines

"I love the Lord with all of my heart, but I have not been living for the Lord. I want to get back close to the Lord like I used to be."

A., Georgia, USA

"I want the Holy Spirit of Jesus."

A., Namibia

"I needed Him all along, and just took a step back and realized all this. Thank you for your little pop-up."

D., West Virginia, USA

"Please help me to have Jesus Christ in my life by helping me to realize that God is good."

G., Philippines (via text message)

"Please help me to know more about Jesus Christ, and help me to realize my purpose in this world and how can I make this world a better place to live in."

C., Philippines

"I just prayed this, and I want to be born again."

K., Nigeria

"As I am studying, I want to know Jesus, I am from a Hindu family and I want to be close to God. Please help."

K., Karnataka, India

"I want to learn everything there is about Christ, and what He wants me to do and how to live. God is the only person that can give me what I need."

E., Guyana

"If we pray hard and repent for our sins, will God forgive us?"

A., India

"Does God love me?"

H., Philippines

"I would like to accept Christ as my Savior."

T., USA

"How can I bring myself to Jesus? How can I hear His call for me?"

M., Philippines

"Please help me to know how to put Christ more as the center of my life. Thanks."

J., New York, USA

"I want to be satisfied, and I want peace in my life."

S., Pakistan

"I would like to dedicate my entire life to Christ. It is in Him that we will find peace."

J., Ghana

"I want Christ to be in my heart and life always. I trust Him in every little way I do. I thank Him for giving me this opportunity to live, and live life again."

L., Philippines

"I would like to be a fully dedicated follower of Christ. I hope this will help me a lots."

B., South Africa

"Thank you for helping me recommit my life to Christ. I really felt discouraged, and felt half hopeless with my dreams, and even my love life. Thank you for that prayer. It really had an impact on my Christian life. I have to trust God! Thank you, and I will continue trusting God—no one else."

N., Philippines

"I love the inspiration of knowing that I can come to Christ, no matter how sinful I may be. Thank you."

G., Nigeria

"That's a wonderful prayer. I've never prayed before. Thanks."

G., Philippines

"I have been trying to run away from God and do things in my own way, but things are not working out for me as I expected. I have realized that I need God to perfect things in my life. Please—I need your prayers and I don't want to look back again. Also, I want things to work out for me in this life. I'm almost tired of this life, but I have faith that God can still perfect things in life because it isn't too late!"

A., Nigeria

"I need Jesus Christ to keep me saved. I don't know; sometimes I just feel afraid of my life. This web is really helping me to realize that Jesus is always here to accompany me! Thank you."

Y., Norway

When I try to pray and tell my heart that Jesus is my Savior in life, I feel a deep peace in my heart. Then, I realize that I have to count on Him on every single day and in every step of my life. Thanks for the beautiful words above."

E., Indonesia

"I need God in my life—I can't stand to be alone any more."

T., Norway

"Thank you for telling me so much about Jesus. Can you send everything about Jesus like you sent this, please?"

H., Chandigarh, India

"This piece that I just read and the prayer I prayed really helped me get my life back on the right track. Thank you very much. And God bless."

M., Western Cape, South Africa

"Thank you for the service. This is all I've been waiting for!"

O., Mozambique

"I was pleasantly surprised to come across this message over this website. May God bless your efforts."

T., Kenya

"Thank you. It's good to know there are still people out there that care."

R., Ohio, USA

"I like the prayer on mobile or on PC. Thank you."

P., Maharashtra, India (via text message)

"Thank you for sharing with me about Jesus."

R., Norway

"Thank you for reminding me about God's love."

T., Gauteng

"With the help of this brief scripture, I have come to understand what life is all about. God bless you."

W., Ghana

"I gave my life to Jesus two years ago, but continued to live in sin. Recently, the Holy Spirit put the church and His word on my heart and I can't get enough of Him. He is so amazing, so glorious and so awesome. Thank you for having a website where others can accept Jesus into their hearts and save their eternal souls. I love everything that has to do with God, so I would love to receive any and all the information that you can provide. Thank you."

E., USA

"I was still separated from my Lord Jesus because of my attitude. Thank you for helping me to return to Christ."

A., Mozambique

"Thank you for being here when people need you."

F., Guyana

"Thank You For being there when I needed You Most! Amen."

A., Michigan, USA

"I thank you for helping me recommit my life to Jesus."

G., Tanzania

"I was logging onto a website and this caught my eye. I've entered into a relationship, and know God must be part of it in order for it to work. We are a couple in love and happy. We speak daily of God and the role He plays, and what He'll do in our future. Thank you so much for ministering in the manner that you have—I know this was God's way of getting through to me!"

A., California, USA

"Thank you for sharing this to all the people who wants to have Jesus in our lives . . . ."

D., Philippines

"Lead me Lord; walk with me always to fight all the odds that comes in life."

C., Dubai, United Arab Emirates

"I am very excited to have come to know this website with such good news. Truly, God is love. Glory be to Him always."

N., South Africa

"Thank you for inviting me to pray this prayer. I pray that God will forgive me for all my wrongdoings, and bless me in a special way. I have problems in my life, and I want to be next to God always."

B., Matsulu

"I am very happy about Global Media Outreach. Indeed, after reading the Four Steps To God, I felt it inside of me, the desire to come back to God. I know it's not easy as in youth to live a life commitment to Christ, but I believe all my prayers will work out for me. Keep praying for me, and Uganda as a whole. God bless this ministry, for it is making Jesus famous in the world."

D., Uganda

"I am very happy that I recommitted myself to Jesus, because He has done a lot in my life."

M., South Africa

"Thank you for making me realize that I am none without God. I want to be committed to God forever. Praise the Lord. Amen."

D., Andhra Pradesh, India

"I'm so confused. I need to know the right road."

D., USA

"I am happy to know that Jesus is my Savior from today, and I pray that God will help me to go on."

L., Kenya

"I want Jesus to come into my life, and to show me the way to how should I lead my life."

J., Orissa, India

"I liked to pray that prayer! What a coincidence! I am in a bad situation! I was looking for something like that!"

L., Mozambique

"I would love to be a real Christian. Help me to become a Christian."

M., Iran

"I would like Jesus to save my life, and help me to leave all sins I have done all my life."

J., Cote D'Ivoire

"I want to know more about the Christ."

C., Mexico

"Thanks to God that I found this website. Maybe this is His way of helping me to know Him better. Honestly, I'm still weak in my faith to Him, especially in a time of trouble. Thank you once more."

M., United Arab Emirates

"Please help me build my life with Christ . . . ."

S., Papua New Guinea

"I was brought up a believer. I thank the Lord for my mother. I accepted Christ into my heart, and first committed my life to Him when I was still a child. Since then, I have strayed away from the word of God many a time. I ask for prayers."

S., Greece

"I accept Christ as my Savior because He died on the cross because of my sin."

G., Sudan

"I am happy to join you and I have been giving myself to Jesus, but I want to see some changes in my life. So please, can you help me so that I can do what I need to do, and also what I want. This is my story."

R., Ghana

"I want to know about your religion."

J., India

"Please, I am a French man and I don't speak good English, but I want to receive Christ in my life."

G., Ghana

"I want to know more about God and His plan for us."

N., USA

"I want to leave this sinful life. Please help me."

M., Punjab, India

"I need to become a more committed and faithful believer. I lost faith when I was at my lowest, and now know how wrong it was of me. That's when I needed to have faith and believe in Him the most. I know that He is with me now and every stage of my life—I just want to be a much stronger believer."

M., Australia

"Now, I'm not yet in Christianity, but I love Jesus. I want to become a Christian."

T., Cambodia

"I really want to understand Christ, and of course in my heart!"

J., China

"I love Jesus. He saved my life—now I am happy with my life. I know He is always with me and helps me out of my tensions. Thanks, Jesus."

A., Pakistan

"I really need to learn more about Jesus, as I was never taught."

S., North Dakota, USA

"Does God really forgive me for things I have done in the past that I am so ashamed and guilty for, even things I haven't told anybody? I haven't even forgiven myself, so how can He forgive me? I don't understand it. I hate myself for it. Does God really love me still, after all that?"

M., North Carolina, USA

"I want more than anything to accept Jesus Christ as my Lord and Savior. He is the reason why my life has changed forever."

B., Ohio, USA

"I accept God as my personal Savior and good Father."

M., Philippines

"I trust the Lord all my life. He has done marvelous things in my life. Praise God! No one has ever loved me like God."

N., New York, USA

"I need you, Jesus! Please help me! I need you to guide me. Help me to get started again! I love you, Lord!"

L., Philippines

"Thank you for putting this website up to help others like me!"

N., Malaysia

"I thank you for this website. I thank you for the prayer of hope in my life again. I let the devil make me think that I was in too much sin for God to hear or bless me. I got out of my bed feeling hurt and so down. But as I type this to you, the Spirit tells my soul not to worry because He will show up on time, and I just thank Him because I feel so much better and I know He is true to His words. Again, I give thanks to this site. But most of all, to my Father God and His son Jesus. Please keep me and my family in your prayers."

T., Georgia

"This website rocks!!! I just recommitted my life the other day, and I wanted to tell someone about it!! Websites like this inspire me!"

L., Texas, USA

"I was surfing the Web and clicked on your website. I thank the Lord for you and your website. Although I am a believer in Lord Jesus, I was encouraged and my faith was strengthened. I will share this website with others, and pray for you. Thank God for you, your family, and ministry."

S., Georgia, USA

"I want to bring my life back to Christ, as I had forgotten Him in times of happiness. I am selfish for only thinking of Him in times of hopelessness. Help me to go back with Him through my soul and my heart, for He is the only one I have for everything. He is my Savior and light to my path—He is everything in this world. So, help me God."

R., Philippines

"I would like to change my life, so I need your help. I really want to grow as a Christian."

F., Dominican Republic

"I want to know more about our Lord Jesus Christ, and love Him. Can you take me to Him?"

K., Ghana

"Jesus Christ is always in my heart. He does everything amazing in my whole life. I love Jesus so much."

M., Indonesia

"Will God help me to rebuild my life?"

A., Tamil Nadu, India

"I love Jesus, and I need His blessing upon me all the days of my life."

A., Nigeria

"I just prayed to receive Christ!"

T., Tamil Nadu, India

"I feel great, and looking forward to experiencing the love of God again."

N., South Africa

"I want to commit my life to Christ."

A., Philippines

"How can I totally receive Christ in my life?"

E., Philippines

"I believe that God exists, and that Jesus redeemed us from our sins. After so many years of striving and failing, I learned how to surrender life to Jesus wholeheartedly. God bless this website."

M., Japan

"I wish to know more about the Holy Spirit."

T., Nigeria

"I want to prosper in life, and have realized that Jesus is the only way—so help me because I am about to do my final college exam. Thank you."

A., Kenya

"How will I know if Jesus really forgives me? My life is hard enough. I don't want any false hopes or promises. How will I know without a doubt that He would want to share in my life? I really want to believe. I need something to hold on to. Please help me—I beg you. I am so tired of feeling alone, lonely, unwanted and unsuccessful. I just want some real meaning in my life. Thank you."

J., Gauteng, South Africa

"I agree that now I accept Jesus to be my Lord."

N., Turkey

"I've been a sinner since I was born. Now I want your help to be born again. Thank you."

M., Kenya

"I want to receive the Holy Spirit."

D., Cote D'Ivoire

"Guide me to let Him be my personal Lord and Savior!"

E., Saudi Arabia

"It's so amazing that in this, I found something that opened my heart to Jesus. Thank you so much."

D., Saudi Arabia

"I want to accept Jesus into my life."

S., Lagos

"I want to learn and accept Jesus and God, and wish to eliminate my sins and be accepted by God."

M., Texas, USA

"I have realized that the way I have been living for the past two years of my life is wrong, and I want to change my ways."

M., Tanzania

"I am interested in becoming a Christian, and am ready to accept Jesus Christ as my Lord and Savior. How can I become a Christian?"

V., Alberta, Canada

"I need the love and mercy of God. And I need Jesus as my Savior."

B., Saudi Arabia

"I want to know Jesus. Please help me on my path to becoming a better father and husband."

J., Michigan, USA

"I feel good about recommitting my life to Christ. I want to be in touch with fellow believers as a way of strengthening my faith in God. All that I am and will ever be I owe to God."

M., Philippines

"I have problems, and I think that only Jesus can save me. What should I do? I really need help."

T., Cameroon

"I want to receive Christ in my life as my Savior. Please pray for me that I change. I want Christ to use me."

M., Zambia

"Your package made me reconsider my spiritual life to be much more important than any other thing in this world."

H., Nigeria

"I belong to a Hindu family. We have been into idol worship. I am the only one in my family who accepted Jesus as my personal Savior and my Lord."

S., Andhra Pradesh, India

"This is wonderful!! Jesus Christ is made available to everyone, anywhere and anytime. May God Bless the work of your hands."

A., Kenya

"I want to know more about Christ because I am Muslim."

M., Essex, UK

"I really want to know Jesus Christ. Please help me."

M., Cote D'Ivoire

"I am just so happy to accidentally open this website. Maybe God had showed me the way to Him."

P., Philippines

"How do I grow my faith in Jesus Christ? How can I faithfully follow Him and obey all His commandments?"

L., Zimbabwe

"How do I live my day-to-day life as a Christian?"

M., Korea

"How could I be a Christian?"

J., France

"What do I have to do to receive Christ in my heart?"

M., China

"How can I be a good Christian?"

D., Taiwan

"What do I do to know Him more?"

O., Nigeria

"How do I increase my relationship with Jesus Christ?"

H., China

"Thanks for just being on the Net. I was just browsing, being lost, and I decided to type in "God" in a search and I found this video. It made my day. I have lived a Christian life when I was smaller. When I got to my teens, I fell out of His hands and into a lost world. Now that I have my children I have found a better life, and it needed more meaning and I know God can help with that. Thanks again for your time. This video can be such a miracle for people, even if it is just a video."

M., Canada

"I want to change my lifestyle and become God's child."

L., Gauteng, South Africa

"I want to know God."

R., Saudi Arabia

"What will I do to be saved?"

T., Italy

"What should I do after receiving Christ?"

B., Tanzania

"God, I need you in my life and I'm so sorry for my sins. Please—please just give me presence of mind always. Thank you so much, Lord."

W., Philippines

"How can I show my love to God?"

A., Malaysia

"Please tell me more about God's Love and the love of Christ."

A., United Arab Emirates

"I want to give my life for Jesus. I love Him truly. I know even in sadness and happiness. It happened because He does really love me."

B., Indonesia

"I don't know what to say for now, but I want to know how to surrender all my life—all my problems—to Christ Jesus?"

R., Kuwait

"I want to know more and more why Jesus died for me and other people?"

E., Tamilnadu, India

"I really want to commit myself to Jesus Christ."

F., Botswana

"What can I do to receive the glory of God?"

S., Ghana

"Thank you very much for hosting this website. I believe that my life will change. I will be in touch with you for more assistance."

R., Tanzania

"I have been having a very difficult time in my life. At this time, I need Christ in my life more then ever before. I am always under spiritual attack by evil spirits. Although my heart is pure, I need God's protection, as well as divine intervention and blessings that I can only receive through the love that Jesus has for me."

L., California, USA

"I have been saved for over a year, and have grown tremendously in just a year. I'm almost done with my Bible all the way through twice, but just wanted to see what else I could learn and if you could help me."

J., Tennessee, USA

"I'm going through things at this point in my life that I feel is trying to overtake me. I need God. I know He is the only one that can take me through it."

C., California, USA

"I asked the Lord to come into my life and take all the sinful things and thoughts I have had. Also, that He would forgive and bless me. I pray. I thank Him for giving me another day to change."

N., Wisconsin, USA

"It's true that accepting Jesus and surrendering our lives to Him can help us grow spiritually."

M., Philippines

"I would like to learn more about the Christian religion and about Jesus."

C., Washington, USA

"I'm married and had committed adultery. I want to ask God for forgiveness, and turn away from my sins and start a new life with Jesus."

S., Seychelles, Africa

"Want to regain my faith and trust in God. How do I do that?"

M., Zimbabwe

"I want to know more about Jesus to have an intimate relationship with Him. I do believe that He is my Lord and Savior, and that without Him I'm nothing."

K., Gauteng, Africa

"Thank you so much for giving us the opportunity to know and find this webpage here on the Internet. I will pray for more people to find this page, and also have the opportunity to be saved, too."

M., Peru

"I'm very bad in relationships, and I'm wondering if God is the source to my true love."

G., Michigan, USA

"Just came across this website. It touched my heart so much that there are great people who spread the good news about Christ, and I appreciate it a lot. God Speed."

K., Philippines

"How can I make my relationship true, grounded and long-lasting with the help of Jehovah?"

T., Zambia

"Can you help me to receive Christ as my personal Savior?
If yes, what can I do?"

D., Ghana

"What should I do to have an intimate relationship with God?"

F., Philippines

"I am so happy to get your website; I have been looking for
an organization that will fill me with the true Word of God.
Thanks."

K., Sierra Leone

"I want Christ to come into my life."

C., Nigeria

"I want be around Jesus, and know much more about the
Jesus."

T., Comoros

"I want to know more about God, and I want to request
help to find out if this is the true religion."

J., Philippines

"I prayed to receive Christ so that Jesus can be with me all the time, and guide me in order to make the right choices."

I., South Africa

"I would like to dedicate my life to Christ, and would like to show Jesus Christ in my life to other people."

P., Tamil Nadu, India

"I will need someone who can assist me to Christ, because here in my country I don't have anybody. I am alone. Thanks."

A., Ghana

"I really want to receive Christ in my life."

T., Cameroon

"If you had received Christ Jesus before, then you went astray, does God consider the life and things you did before you become recommitted?"

Z., Gauteng

"I am new born again. How can I be close to God?"

M., Tarabulus

"How can I strengthen my faith?"

A., Kenya

"Thanks for helping me to recommit my life to Christ. May God bless you all."

J., Nairobi

"Thanks for your points on how we can accept Christ as our Lord. Please keep me in prayer, that I will keep living for Him. Thank you."

Z., Monaco

"Yes, I accept my Christ as my Lord and Savior!"

H., Saudi Arabia

"I worry about death. How can I come to peace with this?"

A., Ohio, USA

"Whenever we sin and ask God for forgiveness, how do we know we are truly forgiven?"

T., Nigeria

"I need to change my life around."

J., California, USA

"I need God so much, but I don't know how I can let the door of my heart to become open to Him. What should I do?"

C., Nigeria

"I am interested in becoming a Christian, and am ready to accept Jesus Christ as my Lord and Savior. How can I become a Christian?"

V., Alberta, Canada

"I want to receive Christ in my life as my Savior—please pray for me that I may change. I want Christ to use me."

M., Zambia

"What should I do to have an intimate relationship with God?"

F., Philippines

"I totally believe that Jesus Christ is my only Savior till the end of the age."

S., Switzerland

"I want to know how it feels to have Christ in my life, and to feel His love and forgiveness."

E., Australia

"I want to live a meaningful Christian life so that people can see Jesus in me."

A., Ontario

"I believed in God for a long time. I want to grow personally, and I want my staff to know Jesus and to grow, as well."

B., Cambodia

"I thank God for you because of this website for which I am happy to have found. I believe I am going to be more equipped in the Word of God."

K., Nairobi

"I want you to help me receive Christ, and to change my life."

C., Cameroon

"I accept Christ in my life as my Savior."

Y., Indonesia

"What can I do to be a child of God?"

S., Mozambique

"It's really wonderful belonging to the Lord. Knowing I have a heavenly Father who cares, despite my rebellious attitude. He still calls me back to Him."

S., Cameroon

"I know Jesus is the only living God. I have strived hard to accept Him, but something holds me back from Him. Please pray for me. I want the Holy God to be everything for me. Please."

A., India

"How do I become a Christian?"

B., Burundi

"I just want my life to be turned back to Jesus, to follow His footsteps, and become a better person inside."

E., India

"How can I continue to walk with the love of God? What are the steps I should take to grow stronger in Christ?"

M., Saint Lucia

"I would like to become a faithful follower of our Lord Jesus Christ."

J., Myanmar

"I want to know HIM better and better."

T., Indonesia

"I am happy because I have received Christ into my life. Pray for me to be faithful to God almighty."

E., Indiana, USA

"Oh, it's good to have Christ in our souls because it's the only way we can see the truth and the light. I thank God for His precious mercy on me because I need Him more than I think."

E., Germany

"I would be pleased to receive Christ's message so I can grow spiritually."

P., Sweden

"I have nowhere to turn, yet I still believe that God did not bring me this far to let me go."

L., China

"I have to say thank you for the opportunity."

M., South Korea

"I want Jesus to come into my life, and lead me in the right path."

A., India

"It's nice to browse the Net and see that there are Christian people who you can talk to, and who lift you up as well. God Bless, and more power to you guys. How I wish to be part of your team."

G., North Carolina, USA

"I'm so thankful that I received this invitation. I'll forward this invitation to all my friends, as there are so many who are in worldly desires."

L., California, USA

"What is God's purpose with my life? I have been searching for a long time."

L., Gauteng

"Thanks to the Lord, our Savior, Jesus Christ. I would like to recommit my life to Him. He loves me and He forgives all my sins. I have repented of all my sins, but I do not have peace in my heart. Please pray for me. Thank you."

T., Dubai

"Thank you for taking the time to share God's message. I am looking forward to hearing more from you soon. It is wonderful to know that some people are still concerned about these last times that we are in. God bless."

D., Jordan

"It feels wonderful after praying to God. It brings such a good and great feeling to my life, that I can't express it."

R., India

"The lines of right and wrong are so blurred in today's society. How do we know if we are doing what God wants us to do?"

M., Cayman Islands

"I thank the Lord for coming into my life."

J., India

"I am already a Christian, only this time, I realized how important it is to grow and nourish my spiritual life with fellowship, and live a life that is centered around the Lord Jesus Christ. And, I would like to know more about how can I serve Him and how really my life be used by God; this I really long for, and only this time I felt this sudden urgency to grow more closer to Him. May you show me some more materials so I can be an effective servant of the Lord. Thank you so much for your program reaching the lost."

M., Philippines

"I would like to surrender my life to God, and praise and worship Him. Help me and pray for me. Thank you, and God bless you."

N., Qatar

"I have always felt empty inside, and now that I have found Christ my life feels complete. Thanks for helping me."

J., Tennessee, USA

"Am so grateful to be in God's hand. I need God to change my life and make me a different person again."

Y., New Zealand

"I pray to receiver Christ; I recommitted my life to Christ. I have lost my closeness to Christ—need to find my way back."

T., USA

"I want to know more about faith and believing."

M., Argentina

"I desperately need Jesus Christ back in the center of both mine and my family's life. There is no peace or happiness in our lives without His presence. He is needed first, before anything or anyone else."

F., New York, USA

"I am young and I need a change now. I accepted Jesus to be my Savior when I was around four, but since then I got sucked into the world of looking up stuff I shouldn't be looking up for my age. I need God's love."

V., Switzerland

"I want to become a Christian—my question is, could you help me please?"

R., Australia

"I need Christ to really help me—if not, the way my life is going now, it's going to end up bad!!!"

J., China (via text message)

"I am a baby Christian; what will I do to make myself fully mature?"

J., North Carolina, USA

"I would like to walk in the life of God, and doing what He wants me to do. I want all the negative things out of my life, and do the works of God."

B., Slovak Republic

"I have done so many wrong things, but I hope God can forgive me."

E., UK

"I accept Jesus Christ is as my Savior."

P., Kuwait

"I think that Jesus is knocking in the door of my life; every day, I think that I need Him more."

J., USA

"I think for the first time I finally have peace. I have always carried guilt from the past, and never really understood I didn't have to do that. I would leave it and go back and pick it up, which brought me in deep depression. Thanks be to God for His mercy and grace, and only the peace that can come from Him and Him alone."

C., North Carolina, USA

"I would like to say thank you so much for helping me to receive Christ in my life."

A., Texas, USA

"I have already received Christ, but I want to keep growing as a Christian."

O., Nigeria

"This is a great website—I have been searching for, and now I found it—I want to grow more into Christianity and keep on searching for heavenly living."

R., Kenya

"I love God, for He loves me and saves me, and He is with me every second in my life. I want to stop worrying and being angry about my earthly problems."

D., Saudi Arabia

"I want to give my life to Christ."

B., Ghana

"I really need Jesus back in my life."

N., China

I am just so happy to receive Christ. It took the hurt that I'm feeling right now, because I know Christ is always there to comfort me."

J., Philippines

"How can I change myself completely? How can I lead a righteous life?"

L., India

"I just prayed to receive Christ as my Lord, and I will love to get more info about God."

W., Sierra Leone

"I want to dedicate my life—my soul and my whole time—with Christ. I do hope He keeps standing along with me; teaching me how to worship Him and following Him in faith."

M., Indonesia

"This is awesome. Really appreciate it, and thank God always. Looking forward for your response."

S., Fiji

"I just gave my life to Jesus Christ as my Savior and Lord; I am ex-Muslim from Islam. I need your help to grow in faith and Jesus' road."

A., Cote D'Ivoire

"I want to be a real Christian. So, tell me the process how to be a Christian."

S., Bangladesh

"How can I be so committed to God in my everyday life? I do face a lot of challenges that seem to draw me away from God. Help me."

O., Norway

"Need to know how to believe in God."

S., Nigeria

"I've always wanted to receive Jesus in my life, but I always seemed to sin; I'm ready!"

L., Texas, USA

"I want to be saved, and be with the Lord and Savior Jesus Christ."

D., Guyana

"Why is it that whenever I try to be good, I end up doing wrong things? Do I stand a chance here?"

R., Kenya

"What must one do, in specific in order, to receive His endless love?"

V., Norway

"I really love your preaching, your words change my life; this is my first time of visiting this website—keep God's work up."

S., Nigeria

"I want to pass on the message to everyone, so that they can do the same to be saved."

K., Jamaica

"I need to practice a real Christianity. Am tied to live a doubting life—please help me!!"

G., India

"I am sinful; I know it is bad, yet I continue do those things. I want somebody to help me; control those mistakes of mine. Thank you"

R., Philippines

"I want to change my life, and have my sins forgiven."

K., USA

"What do people mean when they are saying they are born again? And what's the difference with being baptized and being born again?"

W., Namibia

"I want to commit my life to the hand of Jesus. What will I do to accept Jesus as my Lord and my personal Savior? I need Him in my life."

D., Norway

"I thank you for this message—it has really touched my heart."

N., Kenya

"How can I receive Christ as my Savior?"

A., Ghana

"I just prayed to receive Jesus Christ as my Lord and Savior. I want to commit my life to Jesus."

P., Nairobi

"I was so close to Jesus at one point in time. Then I chose the ways of the world, but I want to get back right with God because of what I learned on your website. So, for this, thanks."

J., California, USA

"I wanted to take this opportunity to let you know that I thank God for your ministry! I have learned so much through this website and the e-mails sent through Global Media Outreach. I have been praying with you and for you, and I will continue to do so. Thanks for helping me learn to pray in God's perfect will, mostly through your website. I have prayed for God to make me Christ-centered instead of self-centered. I gave my life to Christ—I have never been so alive and full of joy in any circumstance. Thank you for your obedience to God!"

Robert, USA

The Discipleship Journey

Right now, more than 2,400 trained missionary volunteers are on the front lines of Jesus 2020. These committed missionaries represent a growing grassroots movement that will, with God's blessing, expand to over 100,000 missionaries by the year 2020.

Every day, Jesus 2020 brings thousands of men and women from around the world into a discipleship relationship with missionaries who answer their questions, encourage them, pray for them, and help them begin walking with Jesus.

Global Media Outreach provides each volunteer missionary with all the training they need, as well as ongoing technical, prayer and personal encouragement.

The Journey for Ella and Her Friend Olga From the Soviet Union

We received her first letter in the middle of January, and since then, we have been corresponding with her on a regular basis. Here is what she wrote in her first letter:

"I've tried to come to God on my own and through various books, but it does not work. I want Jesus to be in control of my life, and I need help in this area."

Several days later, she prayed and trusted Christ with her life. After that, visible changes took place in her life. You can see it through the following excerpts from her letters.

Olga's Relationship With God

" . . . I have started to feel and take in the love of Jesus. I am reading and reflecting upon God's Word, but I often get distracted. I ask Jesus to give me the right understanding of the Bible."

" . . . I found the missing link: God loved, loves, and will always love me with all my faults. I wanted to describe to you how I felt at that moment, and I thought that it was similar to what the prodigal son felt when He returned to His father and realized that He had always been loved! I can't find words to describe the whole range of feelings that I had."

" . . . Ella, I can explain why I am seeking God so intensely. When I was in high school, I saw Jesus in a dream. He was standing at a distance from me and said, "I want you to come to me." I was very surprised to have such a dream because we lived in the Soviet Union and no one talked about God back then. I have never been able to forget that dream. I was searching for Him, but I chose wrong paths. Now, after I met you, I am confident that I am on the right way. I am absorbing His teaching like a sponge, but I am afraid I might lose Him again if I make a mistake."

"I saw a link to your website on a dating site. It was there only once, and after that I never saw it again. I believe Jesus gave me that link. He used my correspondence with a man to help me find you and your help."

"Ella, I want to go to a church where I can hear sermons. I am Orthodox, and in Russian Orthodox churches there are no sermons. Can I attend Evangelical or Protestant churches? I think I would feel more comfortable there."

Olga's Relationship With Her Mother

"Hello Ella! Thanks for writing to me. I need your support. I feel rejected and I can't get rid of this feeling. Since early childhood and until now, my mother has been putting me down and insulting me. She often curses me. I am 40 years old and I still live with her. She says I have no right to get married before she dies, and that my desire to leave her is a sin. She had been drinking all her life, but stopped recently. That did not make our life any better. She has a controlling personality. It has been seared into my mind that I do not deserve good things in life. This makes it difficult for me to believe Jesus with my heart because I think He also does not need me. What am I to do?"

". . . I am just at the beginning of the way, but there is light and peace in my heart. Every day I bless my mother and thank God for her. I can't say that I have great love for her, but she does not irritate me anymore. During the last week she has been different—she did not complain or insult me, and was more quiet than usual. I have no desire to bring back to my mind and to focus on the bad things she did in the past. This is possible only because of Jesus and your prayers for me."

". . . Ella, I have realized that I love my mother very much. All my grievances and accusations against her are gone. My heart is filled with tenderness and a desire to help and protect her. This is amazing. I have found my mother. This reminds me of a feeling that I usually have on the eve of a great holiday."

Olga's Attitude Toward Her Sin

"I know that my anger, cowardice and irritation are also from the devil. I am ashamed to write about these things, but I do have them in my heart. Ella, please let me know how I can ask Jesus to help me get rid of all the dirt that is in me. I am looking forward to hearing from you!"

"Ella, I have started to gain self-esteem. This is different from the pride that I used to have when I felt rejected. I still need to change a lot. I have realized that I am very lazy and try to blame my unhappy life for it. I blame everyone else but me. Today, as I saw this in the light of truth, I felt disgusted that Satan has been trying to influence me this way. But now I have Jesus and I do not need to be afraid of anyone else. It was as if I heard Him say, "Just do it and I will help you." Every day, I learn something new from God's Word—this is great!"

Stories From *Jesus2020* Missionaries

"A young woman in Australia wrote saying she was filled with guilt and not able to "connect" with God any more, since she stepped out of obedience and married a "good man," yet he is Muslim. I encouraged her and assured her that God forgives us when we ask Him. The consequences of our decisions may follow us, but God's grace, through Jesus Christ, is sufficient to carry us. She wrote back: "Thank you so much for all the encouragement and nonjudgmental words. You are like a breath of fresh air. In my six years of marriage I have come across Christians, and not one of them has encouraged me in this way. It has touched my spirit greatly. May God bless you as you bless others." She now attends a women's Bible study, and sees a whole different perspective on how to love her husband with Christ's love."

"I am e-mailing now with a wonderful 19-year-old new believer from South Africa. Her faith is becoming stronger every day. I can see how she is becoming more outspoken for Christ there where she lives. She has adopted me as her "mom" and shares with me as such."

"I have a dear couple from India (young believers) that have been through some rough times regarding his family not accepting the new wife. Believing gossip and rumors about her. As we talked, and prayed, and I encouraged them from God's Word, I can see their faith becoming stronger in knowing that God is in control of this entire situation, and He will have the victory in the end."

"I have been talking with someone who does not believe God is love, does not believe Scripture is the Word of God, would rather believe what man has said about "religion," as false as that is. It is times like this that my heart hurts at how Satan has blinded the eyes of people. I have shared with him all I know to be true, but he refuses to accept it. His refusal will cost him his fiancée because she is a believer and has told him she cannot marry him under these circumstances. I have to let him go, but I grieve for the choice he is making. Hopefully one day he will have his eyes and heart opened to grasp the truth. I will check back on him in a few months and challenge him again, but for now I can simply pray for him."

"I had a contact from India, who did not know Christ, through prayers and by the power of God she is today convinced about Christ. She was the only one who has decided to follow Jesus in her family and that of her in-laws. She had a lot of persecutions from both sides about her "new God" (they said). Her husband was the worst case. She had the greatest torment from him. At one point she almost gave up the fight, but I pressed on. It got to a point where I sent some scriptures to him through her, under the leadership of the Holy Spirit. Today she is so convinced about Christ, and her husband today is believing Christ. Other friends and relatives of hers sent their prayer requests to me through her. She was to have her baptism after Easter. Praise God today she is bringing others to Christ and asking for advice often."

"Another case was that of a homosexual who was so addicted to it and found nothing absolutely wrong with that. He argued, despite all my attempts to point out through scriptures that it was wrong. I kept on, and after a while he wrote a four-page e-mail of true confession, which he has never told anyone as he said. He had been with 96 men, and he finally repented. Praise God. The experiences are so many that I can't write all; but I must, with all my heart, thank God for this wonderful opportunity He has given me to share Christ with others."

"I had a lady who was about to have an abortion, but after visiting our website talked to her partner and they are getting married and raising the child—what a great change of heart and mind—thanks to the Lord's calling her to the website."

"I have a man in Kenya that was suicidal, and had no one to share his story with. He felt comfortable sharing it with me and now feels God's forgiveness, and is living his life for Christ and writing beautiful praise songs (which he sends me the lyrics to periodically)."

"I have been writing to an older gentleman from an island near Malta for several months. When he first contacted me, he wanted to know how to be a good Catholic. We have had some great discussions about grace and forgiveness. His wife was dying of cancer (and recently passed away), and he has been reading some of the online material I've directed him to. He has been so grateful for our conversations and for the information—it's humbling to be used by God in this man's life."

"I have gained a new friend in Nigeria, who when he first contacted me was looking for encouragement in his faith . . . we talked about some of his concerns, and I was able to encourage him in the work that he wanted to do in his homeland . . . . He since has gotten married to a lovely Christian girl, and they now have a 1-year-old little boy . . . in all this, I have been able to share and encourage both him and her as they started their family."

"I have had quite a few who obviously have been genuinely converted, and give wonderful stories of faith and changed lives. I have seen many people come to faith in Christ. I have encouraged them to grow in their faith through the online Bible study course offered, and to encourage each one to get involved in a solid local church."

"I was e-mailing a man in the Middle East. He had many questions about who God is and why He cared about us. We went back and forth several times. He hasn't yet received Christ, but I think God is working in his heart."

"I was in contact with a family in Cameroon. They shared with their Bible Study Group information I sent about evangelism. The group eventually went to surrounding villages in outreach."

"I've been able to have a great friendship with Zenaida, who lives in Saudi Arabia. She doesn't have a church she can go to because of where she lives. I've given her several things she can do at home. She wrote me the other day saying,

"Every time I receive one of your letters, it makes me cry."
What a blessing."

"I've been dealing with a fairly young lady that has been diagnosed with probably terminal cancer. She has a good husband and three children. Have shared from my own experience with cancer, and have a dialogue of offering prayer and comfort."

"Have two people from India that accepted Christ. They are working to enroll in a Bible school to get training so they can go back to their own villages and spread the Word."

"I've had an ongoing ministry of encouragement, teaching, and, to an extent, mentoring and discipleship with a young man in Malaysia named Tan."

"It has been great to hear occasionally from one guy who has had success battling pornography, or to hear about those who have accepted Christ even though they are in Muslim countries."

"It's been mostly people who are on the brink of suicide, they tell you they have tried everything, and I am their last hope before departing from this world. Initially I would not sleep, in fear of me not saying the right thing and never hearing from them again. Every single one of them are so inspired again—the Lord proves that He is alive and omnipresent, He hears every call and answers every prayer."

"Mphatso became a Christian when he was 16, and his Muslim father kicked him out of the house. Around that time, his mother died of a witchcraft incident. He went to live at the church where the pastor took him in. He logged onto one of our websites, and I encouraged him, sent him a Bible in his own language. He lives only to reach the country of Malawi for Christ, and has become the leader of the youth in his church, organizing short mission trips. He is 21 years old, on fire for Christ. The Four Spiritual Laws were published online in his language, but not printed or sold anywhere. I got the rights to print it here in my city from CCC, and printed tracts to send to him. He uses them in outdoor meetings and in traveling evangelism, and orders more from time to time. He has reached many, many people in Malawi where the gospel did not go before. He is a growing leader, and communicates with me weekly."

"Niry, from Kenya, e-mailed that she had received the Lord as her Savior for the first time. I prayed about it, then asked her some questions about her new life and new faith. I told her it is very important to find a Bible teaching church, and to follow the Lord in believer's baptism. She responded back several times. She stated she had found a Bible teaching church and had been baptized. She also stated that she had joined a Bible study group. This girl makes my heart sing. I pray for her continually, and send her notes of encouragement from time to time."

"One man told me that he felt that there was no one out there for him; he said that he had sent e-mails to multiple websites and no one answered any of his questions. But now that I answered, he feels that he is not alone and that there is someone out there who cares and who is praying for him!"

"One married man in his twenties was struggling with his wife and marriage. Through our e-mails he was encouraged to repent of infidelity in his life, and to focus on trusting God with his marriage again. We e-mailed for several weeks and he seemed encouraged. And I have not received an e-mail from him recently, so only God knows how this young man has grown closer to Jesus."

"One of my first contacts was with a young lady in Georgia who apparently was possessed. She couldn't sleep at night because she kept seeing demons. She gave her life to Christ. My community leader helped in finding her a church that would be willing to help and pray over her. In her last letter, her language sure changed. I could tell she had a love of Jesus in her heart, and total faith in Him. She goes to church regularly."

"Recently, an inquirer named James has been e-mailing me regularly, for about the past five months, with questions about Christianity, the Bible, and many such things. He is a Christian, but was in "bad shape" when he first e-mailed. I have seen him grow a lot through the kinds of questions he has e-mailed, and his responses. He seems to have grown from being a confused, wandering Christian, to a thinking, confident, serious Christian. I have become truly excited about what God is doing in his life."

"There's a person on the East coast who has sent me many e-mails and sounded very down, and as I give her more scripture each time to learn and memorize, she is now asking how she can pray for me!"

"One person, Lawrence, asked the simple question: 'Is Jesus God?' This could have been just a taunt, but I felt the Holy Spirit leading me to take it seriously. What to do: To really answer this simple question, I would need to go into a lot of detail; however, that runs the risk of being too much to read and losing what looked like a true open door to an unbeliever's heart. I lead a Lighthouse (small group adult Bible study), and decided to discuss this question. It was a fantastic discussion, and the next day I responded with a two-level response—first a simple answer, Yes, followed by more detail, including a number of Bible references. I was pleasantly surprised to receive a response a few days later. He had studied the material in depth, and responded with a barrage of other questions, which appeared to be stimulated by discussions with Muslims, Catholics and Mormons. Clearly this person was sincere. Over several additional e-mails totaling over 20 pages single-spaced text, I responded to his questions with additional information and many Bible references. Finally, he acknowledged that Jesus is God and it was time to convert this "head knowledge" to "heart knowledge." I gave him my testimony about how I realized I was a sinner and asked him if he felt the same way, and if he did, now was the time to confess his sin to God, accept God's gift of salvation through Jesus' death on the cross. He responded back that he had prayed the prayer. We are still communicating, and he has additional spiritual questions. Now he needs to get plugged into a church and develop some face-to-face fellowship with believers."

"One lady in my age range who never married, and says she feels lonely. I have another ministry of writing devotional e-mails, and I have put some of those in my response e-mails to help her in her walk with Christ. She seems to really like that. She said that she is reading God's Word, even if it's just a few verses a day. She has health problems and identifies with me because I had a kidney and liver transplant seven months ago. She has diabetes and suffers from depression at times, and I am able to encourage her through God's Word."

"There is a gentleman in India who prayed to receive Christ for the first time. He'd read the Bible before and struggled with passages (like Matthew 12:30–32, which talks about the unpardonable sin). After reading my explanation of that passage, he felt encouraged and feels comfortable asking me questions."

"There was someone who lost hope and couldn't talk to anybody. Was depressed, but didn't know where to go, because he was ashamed since he was poor. After talking to me, he started to realize that his life has been blessed; and even though he doesn't have Internet connection, he's still trying to connect to the Internet whenever possible to e-mail me."

"Most amazing, though, is just opening my inbox and realizing that each day another person has put their faith in Christ. So many have thanked me for telling them about Him. Many are so grateful for the 30-day study."

Global Media Outreach
Ministry Distinctives

- *Jesus2020* is using worldwide media technology—not only to share the gospel—but also to make a safe human connection that leads a new believer into a caring relationship with a Christian friend who has received specialized training in faith-sharing and discipleship.

- We help our partners reach searching people in the major Internet trade languages through a massive network, 24 hours a day, seven days a week, 365 days a year.

- All new believers who have received Jesus as Savior are supported by a worldwide prayer network.

- With God's blessing, *Jesus2020* is reaching people in every nation, requiring only the funding partners to generate an ever-increasing flow of searching visitors to our websites.

- By God's grace, and with the help of our volunteer missionaries, we have doubled our evangelism and discipleship each year.

- All Internet and cellular platforms are renewable resources, continuing to do evangelism and discipleship year after year.

- We use a proven security system that protects both the person who is searching and the missionary who is providing help to new believers.

- Our partners are provided with verifiable reports of exactly what their investments are accomplishing. Global Media Outreach reporting shows actual statistics from those who visit, those who indicate decisions for Jesus, and those who request follow-up.

- Based in Silicon Valley, Global Media Outreach, has top executive connections with leading technology companies and venture capitalists. We are on the cutting edge of global communications technology.

The proven communication platforms of *Jesus2020* have the potential to draw millions—yes—scores of millions of men, women, and young people into the Kingdom every moment of every day, for decades to come.

"I am the vine, you are the branches; he who abides in Me and I in him, he bears much fruit; for apart from Me you can do nothing."

— John 15:5 —

Jesus2020

Giving Every Person On Earth Multiple Opportunities To Know Jesus

Can you hear the cry of these searching hearts? Time after time, they simply say, "Help me." "Please help me find forgiveness, acceptance, freedom from guilt." "Please help me find the peace and love of God."

And then to hear them say, over and over, "Thank you. Thank you for leading me to our loving Father and His beautiful Son Jesus Christ."

So many times they reach out, saying, "Please pray for me."

It is up to us, the followers of Jesus, to do everything we can to boldly proclaim the message of His life, truth, and hope to those who are still searching. We must offer friendship and encouragement to help new believers take root and grow up in Christ, becoming fruitful laborers for the Glory of God.

Our God is worthy of our every effort to give every person on earth multiple opportunities to know Him, the ONE who poured out His life for us ALL. Join us on this journey to make His name known and loved among every people, in every nation, everywhere, by the year 2020.